Sardinia: The Undefeated Island

On the road from Santa Margherita di Pula to Teulada

Sardinia
The Undefeated Island

*

MARY DELANE

FABER AND FABER
London: 24 Russell Square

First published in mcmlxviii
by Faber and Faber Limited
24 Russell Square London WC1
Printed in Great Britain by
The Bowering Press Plymouth

Acknowledgment

I have to thank officials of the *Ente Nazionale Italiano per il Turismo* and of the *Ente Sardo Industrie Turistiche* for their kind assistance. And in particular Doctor Salvoni, Delegate for Great Britain, Mr John Greenwood, the ever helpful Press Officer, and Signor Eliseo Meloni, himself a Sard, all of the London office of ENIT for their encouragement and goodwill without which my journey would have been even more difficult. The same could and should also be said of Signor Bruno Piredda, of the Nuoro office of *Ente Provinciale per il Turismo*, whose kindly help made so much difference—all the difference, in fact, between looking from the outside in, and the inside out.

My thanks are also due to Messrs Longmans, Green & Co. Ltd. for permission to quote from Professor G. M. Trevelyan's *Garibaldi and the Thousand*, and Messrs William Heinemann Ltd. for permission to quote from D. H. Lawrence's *Sea and Sardinia*. And that I owe a further debt to John Warre Tyndale for his encyclopaedic survey, *Sardinia*, I gratefully acknowledge.

M.D.

Contents

9

Plates

SARDINIA

0   10   20   30   40
Miles

Straits of Bonifacio
Santa Teresa
La Maddalena
CAPRERA I.
Santo Stefano
Palau
Arzachena
San Pantaleo
Punta Sardegna
S. Maria di Neve
Calangianus
Olbia
Golfo d'Aranci
Golfo di Olbia
GALLURA
Aggius
Tempio
M.te
P. Balestrieri
Monti
S. Teodoro
Perfugas
Nulvi
Limbara
Oschiri
Sorso
Sennori
Osilo
Ozieri
Sassari
Ploaghe
Sinibola
Bitti
ASINARA I.
Golfo
dell' Asinara
P. del Falcone
Stintino
Castel Sardo
Porto Torres
Ittiri
Thiesi
Bonnanaro
Torralba
Giave
Bonorva
Orune
Orune
Cedrino R.
Orosei
Capo Caccia
Alghero
Nuoro
S. Giovanni
Dorgali
Golfo
Cala Gonone
di
Bosa
Tinnura
Macomer
Oliene
M. Tiscali
Grotta del
Bue Marina
Orose
Tresnuraghes
Mamoiada
Orgosolo
C. di Monte Sant
Cuglieri
Santu
Lussurgiu
Ollolai
Fonni
Fontana Bona
Santa Caterina
Paulilatino
Gennargentu
Tonara
Bruncu Spina
Mountains
Arbatax
Sorgono
Desulo
Capo Bellavis
Belvi
La Marmora
Villanova
Strisaili
Tortoli
Aritzo
Lanusei
Oristano
Seulo
Bari Sardo
S. Giusta
Laconi
Arborea
Gesturi
Terralba
Uras
Lasplassas
Barumini
Sanluri
Flumendosa
Guspini
Villa-
santa
Furtei
Villacidro
Serrenti
Muravera
Domusnovas
Monastir
R. Cannas
Iglesias
Decimomannu
Quartu
Siliqua
Elmas
Portoscuso
Carbonia
Capoterra
CAGLIARI
Mortorius
Geremeas
Villasimius
Carloforte
Giba
Orbetto
Golfo di
Cagliari
Capo Carbonara
I. DI S. PIETRO
Calasetta
S. Antioco
Sant'Anna
Arresi
Sarroch
Nora
Pula
S. Margharita
Domusdemaria
I. DE S. ANTIOCO
Teulada
Monte
Maria
Capo Teulada
Capo Spartivento

Part One
*
GALLURA

I heard the remark first in London, later in Sardinia itself. None of the speakers was trying to impress me. '*Ma, la Sardegna non è mai stata vinta*', they said. 'But Sardinia was never defeated.'

It was a gallant statement, made, not boastfully, but quietly as accepted fact. And if, particularly since the unification of Italy in 1860, and following two World Wars, this is not wholly correct in terms of modern politics, nonetheless it remains true in essence, as any real contact with the indomitable, forthright *Sardi* makes plain. In their hearts they never have been vanquished, their known history shows that.

A small, mountainous island situated strategically in the western Mediterranean, only about 150 miles long and some 75 miles from east to west at the widest point, almost equidistant from the European mainland and from North Africa, for more than 2,000 years Sardinia was repeatedly invaded and pillaged, its people carried off in thousands to slavery and death. But time and time again the Sards came down from their mountain hide-outs in revolt against their successive enemies, refusing to remain subjugated.

John Warre Tyndale, an English barrister, who wrote a three-volume survey, *The Island of Sardinia*, more than a century ago refers, indeed, to a legend that the islanders would never suffer defeat, and quotes as authorities Aristotle, Pausanias, Pliny and Silius Italicus among others.

*   *   *

As we waited with varying degrees of patience in the stifling mid-day heat of early Roman summer for the plane to take us on to our destinations a Sardo couple put it in a nutshell. Did I know Sardinia, they asked, but how well did I know its people? *'Sono molto fieri, ma anche molto ospitali.'* 'They are tough, but they are very hospitable.' And that last word was intended in the widest sense.

The day that had dawned so cheerfully, as the beginning of a fascinating if exacting journey, was deteriorating fast. At London airport, after several postponements, it was presently announced, in a tone of voice suggestive of a reward to the class for good conduct, that a change of plane had been made, that passengers to Rome on British European Airways, Flight number so and so would now travel in a Trident. Well, that was fine as far as I was concerned. It is a splendid plane, giving a wonderful impression of power and dignity, as well as being comfortable. We were embarking at last, grumblers stopped grumbling, stray baggage, stray children were all gathered and we set off for the aircraft. At which point the zip of my bulging briefcase gave up the ghost. Books, papers, maps, letters and even paper clips were spewed out over an unbelievable radius, to be rescued with the kindly help of BEA staff and fellow passengers, including a small boy who, with a captivating smile of commiseration offered one of my notebooks with a bonus of a half finished ice lolly. 'For you', he said comfortingly.

Soon the toy-town look of houses and traffic lanes gave place to the wider lands of France, and at last to the serene dignity of the whitecapped Alps with their tiny green villages far below. Above was the brilliance of an almost cloudless summer day. Problems and irritations dropped away with that splendid euphoria engendered by feeling utterly divorced from reality by time and distance. But the day was not yet done.

Something was amiss at Rome airport. That was immediately evident. And that there were a lot of cross and confused people about. But very rapidly sheep and goats were separated as far as we were concerned, passengers for Sardinia and other Alitalia domestic airlines were bundled without more ado into a vehicle and taken to the appropriate building, a comparatively very Spartan affair. There we were dumped and the sad truth emerged: there was a strike in protest against the threatened dismissal of some 80 employees, a strike that might, we felt, perhaps spread. Bars, shops and other services were non-existent.

We sat, and sat, and sat, in a furnace or so it felt, large, open doors letting in with the heavy air all that was worst of the noise and smell of engines being tested immediately outside. Three irrepressible Italian children played games that involved wild shrieking and running round and round the rows of seats, hapless, drooping passengers trying vainly to keep their feet out of the way of the unrestrained, charging young. With the help of a hip flask a Cockney taking the missus abroad got very red in the face and I wondered vaguely if a doctor was within easy call. Close to me sat a *Sardo* couple returning on holiday from the United States to which they had emigrated, an aura of triumphant prosperity invading their now damp plumpness. Both wore tight check suits, in the lapel of the wife's jacket two large mauve imitation orchids quivered with the weight of diamanté, as did the veil of the typical American matriarchal crown of little bows and petals perched on bright red hair. Crocodile shoes and handbag and white kid gloves were the gorgeous complement, and the band on the man's cigar was emphatically golden. They were wonderful, larger than life, so happy, so triumphant, so full of kind plans for the family they had not seen for eleven long years. This was their first real holiday and they hoped to stay for six months. In the course of conversation I hazarded a question as to the whereabouts of *bambini*, and could have kicked myself. The woman just looked at me imploringly, dumb, stricken, tears dimming great, dark eyes. Her husband shifted in his seat. '*È morto*', he replied sadly, and took his wife's hand. We changed the subject.

On arrival eventually at Alghero the welcome was marvellous to see, everybody was kissing everybody, everybody was weeping and everybody was so happy. Dreams had come true, or nearly.

The family piled themselves and much baggage into a cavalcade of cars and departed in clouds of dust and glory, but obviously my dreams were not coming true. There was no car waiting for me to drive away, as arranged, no sign of the hire company's representative, no taxi, and no response to an Alitalia official's kindly efforts to telephone the car office in Alghero some seven kilometres away. Soon it would be dark. I was a stranger and alone, I said, and I had to leave early on the morrow, what was I to do? From the general hubbub that arose, each individual with a different suggestion of how best to help, a small man detached himself. He was returning to Alghero, would the *Signora* care to accompany him to the Hertz car company's office? Indeed I would, though it was precisely in the opposite direction that I wished to go, but Mario Secchi's typical Sard generosity extended to the point of finding the missing manager of the car firm, for none of which services would he accept more than my grateful thanks. The error apparently lay with London through a misunderstanding about the date of my arrival, and though it was after hours Gabriele Maresca, the young manager, did his best to redeem the situation by conducting me to my destination, as far from the airport on the opposite side as Alghero.

At the Hotel dei Pini: oh, no, *signora*, they had no reservation for that name, none at all, nor any accommodation available. They were very, very sorry, but . . . Weary and hungry I stood my ground and presently the missing letter was found amid a flurry of apologies, room and bath had been reserved, and after a further interval of an hour during which one of my suitcases was missing everything sorted itself out.

*   *   *

Though snow may lie on the highest peaks of the Gennargentu mountains in the central province of Nuoro for as long as five months of the year, Sardinia generally has about nine months of sunshine, and the following day was no exception.

Standing in its own grounds among the pine trees, as the name suggests, at the edge of a private beach, the Hotel dei Pini faces Alghero the other side of the bay, on this lovely morning across an expanse of pale, shimmering blue, a gentle lapping at the water's edge like the soft rustle of silk, and the faint chirrup of small birds the only sounds in the clear light of early day.

Alghero is on the extreme west of the island; my immediate objective, still in the north, but on the east coast, was Olbia, and I set out as directed, Ploaghe and Oschiri en route having been carefully marked for me on my map. 'Skirt Sassari', I was told, 'just beyond, at the top of the hill take the right fork, not the one on the left marked "Olbia". The one on the right is an *autostrada*, the one on the left a *strada bianca*, not on the map yet, only just finished, very good. But take the *autostrada*.'

Obeying instructions I took the right fork. True enough it led to a fine new *autostrada* dropping in a series of hairpin bends to open rolling country, tall eucalyptus trees and poplars sometimes bordering the road, shading hedgerow flowers, ripening or recently cut corn a deep golden brown on either side, interspersed with untilled lands dotted with clumps of the ubiquitous cistus, lentisk, myrtle and small evergreen oaks—the famous *macchia* of the island.

I had yet to discover that Sard road signs are not yet always on a par with the excellent conditions of the main highways themselves, but are inclined to a waywardness, and it was presently borne in on me that while signposts continued to indicate the way to Macomer, almost due south, there was no suggestion of any turning to Olbia, and that I needed to be travelling eastward. After some cogitation and a few more hopeful miles I decided to go back to that fork. At least the other road did say 'Olbia'. So, back at the fork, I took the left, and very soon found myself on the vaunted *strada bianca*, in *Sardo* terms, an unasphalted way. It was *bianca* all right, and certainly new, so new that for some distance it was not even rolled. Promising, yes, but its final condition far from being achieved. I crawled carefully and bumpily along, clouds of dust rising behind me, and though I slowed down still more to pass them, an unfortunate shepherd and his flock were almost engulfed. I called a greeting and apologies, but with a grin the *pastore* waved me on. It didn't matter, he said, yes, this was the road to Ploaghe. And in no time there it was, to the left, and after it, Oschiri, small, grey stone villages, neither distinguished, the road continuing through a wide and lovely valley beneath the

rugged granite ridges of the Limbara range, on to a gently un-
dulating plain bounded on three sides by mist-shadowed mountains, to Olbia on the eastern seaboard.

It didn't raise my ego to learn on arrival that if I had continued on the original *autostrada* for another couple of miles or so
I should have found a turning marked 'Olbia'. Next time I
would know.

One of the most ancient ports in Sardinia, Olbia is also the
most important not only in Gallura, but in the whole northern
province of Sassari by virtue of its proximity to the *continente*, the
Sardo name for the Italian mainland. It is a pleasant, undis-
tinguished little town, the centre on a crest of a slight rise,
narrow roads dropping away on all sides except the *piazza*, and
from there the view is blocked at the end. Not only are there no
important buildings to be seen from this point, but there is no
vista at all, the life of the town to some extent divided by the
fact that the port itself is down the hill, the main quays
away to the left. The rather negative impression could also
be caused by the fact that the area has been ravaged so
many times by different invaders, and its people so debilitated
by the disastrous *intemperie*, the island name for malaria, so long
the scourge of the whole of Sardinia, that they had little energy
left for the task of rebuilding their town as well as their lives.

The early history of Sardinia has never yet been precisely
established, records and opinions sometimes differing. Whether
the first traders or colonists were Greeks, who gave the island
the name of Ichnusa, by which it was once known, or its other
version, Sandaliotis, because of the resemblance in terms oʃ
shape to a man's sandal, is not certain, nor whether the Lybians
under Sardus were previous rivals. Of the original inhabitants
still less has so far been determined. By the same token, Olbia,
meaning happy, is thought to indicate early Greek occupation,
though as Tyndale points out with gentle cynicism and some
reason, it was in the event something of a misnomer.

Phoenicians who established early trading centres in the south
were driven out by Greeks, these by the aggressive Carthaginians who ravaged and pillaged, and were themselves defeated

by the Romans. In the year 259 B.C. Scipio leading his troops sacked Olbia, carrying thousands of luckless Sards from Gallura to Rome as his prisoners, to be shown in his Triumph, and shortly afterwards Sardinia became the first Roman province. Ousting Romans eventually came the Vandals. Later, Byzantines, Saracens, Pisans, Genoese, Spaniards and Austrians all took their toll.

During fighting between Pisans and Genoese the little town of Olbia was once more destroyed, to be rebuilt by the former in the twelfth century as Terranova, by which name it was still known when D. H. Lawrence visited it in 1921.

Until recently Gallura was one of the poorer regions, the less formidable coastline of the south and west facilitating trading incursions as well as other invasions more easily.

Now, thanks to two quite different and peaceful invasions, Gallura is enjoying a period of material prosperity such as it has never previously known. The first of these onslaughts, from which the whole of Sardinia has benefitted, was the campaign to exterminate the malaria mosquito. This was begun with a limited experiment in 1943 restricted to Arborea, and was started by UNRRA (the United Nations Relief and Rehabilitation Association). Four years later, from 1947 to 1952, thanks to the generosity of the Rockefeller Foundation of America which financed the project, joint American, Sard and British teams, from a headquarters in Cagliari, undertook a systematic exploration of the entire island, of every town and village, of marshland, pool and valley, of every possible source of danger, indoors and out, from the pest that had for so long been the national plague. Doorposts, buildings, walls of all kinds carry the trade mark of these efforts, the letters DDT, and date of application of the chemical used for the spray. Subsequent dates confirm the resolution of Sard authorities to continue the good work, and a new generation now being born is likely to bear witness in terms of good health as the first without the taint of this enervating fever in the blood. Already in the sturdier appearance of teenagers, with less of the infection in their blood, in their clearer eyes and brighter skins, by contrast with the sallow countenances and listless air of many of the previous generations, is to be seen the beginning of a new and more vigorous island life.

A Sard who had been a member of one of the Rockefeller teams told how, attacked by the disease at the age of three months, he was six years old before he could walk, and was carried to school by a sister. 'I was very proud to have been enrolled to help. It was almost a siege, and took quite a time to make the older generation understand the benefit of what we were trying to do. To get them to accept the injections took quite a lot of persuasion, sometimes it turned skins bright yellow, and people thought they were being given the plague. But now they understand, and are glad.'

Reading the literature of earlier writers referring to the lethargy then prevalent makes interesting comparison with what is now evident in the developing vitality of a whole people so pitifully and desperately hampered in their long and bitter past by an evil of which they neither knew the cause nor the cure.

The second and even more recent invasion, particularly applicable to Gallura, is represented by the enormous investment of foreign capital in terms of the development of tourist facilities, the most important being in the region of Arzachena, just north of Olbia, where an international consortium at present headed by the young Aga Khan has bought several hundred acres of land, including some 35 miles of unbelievably beautiful coast, now known as the *Costa Smeralda*. Five first-class hotels have already been built, villas, shops, a deep water yacht basin, roads and other services. At the time of writing this book the capital investment was quoted as being about £30 million; in fact, discussion with some of the original participants in the scheme suggests a figure nearer £50 million, which is a lot of money in any currency.

The consortium express themselves as prepared to take 15 years over development, and certainly the skill and taste with which much of the work has been done is an outstanding example of the virtue of planning when it is well done, with the aid of such men as the architects Michele Busiri Vici of Rome, and the Frenchman, Jacques Couelle.

Already, and inevitably, the area is not without its anecdotes. The story of Princess Margaret's leap overboard from the Aga Khan's yacht in 1964 is still told with keen interest, and details will no doubt grow with the years. The version recounted to me by a man present was that the boat was holed on a rock coming in, and the captain was trying to beach it when a French boat, offering to help, threw ropes aboard the damaged craft that was slowly sinking in the shallow water. Had such aid been accepted it is possible that legal questions might have arisen on the subject of salvage, other considerations apart. This might have involved the value of personal property of passengers who, in this case, included not only the Princess, but other rich women as well, all possessing, perhaps, luggage of considerable value. Possibly partly on this account, argument is said to have waxed strong, the Aga Khan's captain drew his knife and cut the French ropes, amid a certain amount of general confusion. And probably thinking the most sensible thing to do was to get out of the way, Princess Margaret, who is an excellent swimmer, dived overboard and swam the short distance to the shore with other passengers, including her husband, Lord Snowdon. The news is reported to have been telephoned to London by a quick-witted English model girl then working in one of the local shops.

Be that as it may, the unprecedented development of the *Costa Smeralda* has resulted in labour flooding in from other areas, as well as improved incomes for the already established families in Olbia, to the extent, according to one man closely connected with the trade, that the population had doubled in the last five years and that there are now more cars per capita in Olbia than in Milan. And though this sudden, unforeseen change in so many lives after generations of privations may not always be wholly beneficial, at least, as one resident put it, 'little boys don't go down to meet the ferries any more, trying to flog their grandfathers' land'.

There is a dry twist to this side of the situation. Previously, on the death of the head of a family the land has always been apportioned in such a way that the youngest, or perhaps the least favoured son, has been given the coastal strip, regarded more or less as worthless consisting as it does mostly of rocks, sand and scrub. This has now become the most valuable territory, fetching the highest prices, with a resulting *volte face* in terms of power in a family.

In the town of Olbia itself, of the Roman wall that once surrounded it few traces remain, and on the outskirts is the church of the martyred San. Simplicio, a Pisan building replacing an earlier edifice in memory of the saint whose Feast Day is still the occasion of an important annual celebration.

In the heart of the town the *parrochia*, the parish church, is partly enclosed by a wall, and only the shining, round, variegated tiles of the dome indicate its whereabouts until one is almost on it. I tried unsuccessfully to enter. Watching my efforts a girl standing in a doorway opposite came across to help, but she, too, failed, then a man joined us with no better success, by which time several had gathered. If the *signora* wanted to see their church, why she should, and there were pleased smiles all round when a small unlatched door was finally found. This was typical, travelling over the whole island I rarely needed help of any kind that was not immediately forthcoming in abundant measure. A situation reported also by Tyndale with pleasure 120 years ago. '. . . Though aware of the Sard character for hospitality it far exceeded my expectations . . .'

Inside the *parrochia* beautifully carved choir stalls of a rich, dark wood were lovely, and at a small organ a young man sat playing, absorbed, oblivious of the stranger quietly standing in the shadows. He played very well indeed, but after a brief wait I crept quietly away, fearful of disturbing his concentration, and wandered down to the port. There, the main jetty stretches a long arm into the sea, and at one side an overnight ferryboat plying to and from Civitavecchia was tied up. Owned by the Tirrenia Company these ships are a good size, comfortable, clean and well organized. I had travelled by this means on a previous visit and found the experience wholly satisfactory.

At the far end of the port a Russian ship was unloading timber for pulping at an Olbia factory recently very much in the news when the young manager, Signor Palazzini, had been abducted and held for ransom. He was later released, unharmed, but re-percussions were considerable and widespread. I heard it sug-gested that earlier politics were involved, but this was never confirmed, and no arrest had then been made.

On the opposite side of the jetty the famous mussel beds were being tended. This is a long-established industry, but though the coasts of the island abound with excellent fish the Sards are not, on the whole, great fishermen, presumably owing to the fact that hundreds of years of successive invasions deterred them from trying to establish themselves on any considerable scale in this trade. Rather, for safety's sake, they build their homes away from the coasts, wherever possible in the leeward side just below the top of a peak, offering a commanding view on a site difficult for foes to reach.

A good export market for shellfish expecially is now develop-ing on the mainland, for which reason such delicacies are not always easy to obtain in Sardinia itself; when they are they are fairly expensive.

Tunny fishing is quite another proposition, skilled, dangerous, well organized and profitable, mostly run by the Genoese com-panies who provide the considerable capital required for the canneries. The two main fisheries at Stintino, on the extreme north-west, and at San Pietro, the extreme south-west, being dependent on the wholly unpredictable direction each spring of the great fish as they storm through in their thousands on the way to spawning grounds in the Black Sea.

Water, or rather the lack of it at times, is still a problem in Olbia, aggravated one would think by failure for one reason or another to install cisterns not only in older houses, but in modern ones as well, the result being that shortages are immediately felt. So it was the day after my arrival. The *Sirocco* had started to blow, storm clouds to gather, and in the heavy air we inevi-tably felt limp and sticky, shut among a group of houses in the centre of the town. The situation was not improved when Anne Bassett, my hostess, suggesting a bath, found that the water had already been turned off—the first thing in the morning! For several days previously it had been turned off in the afternoon;

that could be endured with a little organization and some restraint, but so early in the morning with no indication when it would be resumed was not a happy prospect. One wondered about families with small babies, and about the hospital. Meanwhile we decided to give it best and go over to Golfo d'Aranci for lunch.

On the outskirts of Olbia to the north lie the salt marshes, now drained in part for building purposes. Beyond, as the road rises, the view is lovely. All along this fretted coastline gaunt rocks raise their huge grey heads among stunted, windswept trees and dark, evergreen scrub. Below, in small, empty, sheltered bays dazzlingly white sand stretches far out into limpid blue-green water so clear that even small ridges in the sea floor are visible at depths of 30 and 40 feet.

The little village of Golfo d'Aranci, tucked into the northern end of the Golfo di Olbia, was in the throes of a building boom, and here the Sard partiality for brightly-coloured houses, or at least door and window frames, was manifest. Vivid greens, pinks and reds were shock colours among gentler apricots and yellows, softened in some measure by old, lichen-wrapped dry stone walls lining the route and sometimes the little gardens rioting with prodigal growths of bouganvillia, oleanders, fuschia, roses, lilies and other flowers among the darker green of rosemary, their scent mingling with that of the thyme and cistus in the wilder countryside beyond.

Built only a few years ago the Margherita is listed as a second class hotel, a category not by any means to be despised. The classification of Italian hotels both in the island and on the *continente* is a somewhat complicated affair involving all sorts of details not easily understood by laymen, but both in Calabria and here in Sardinia I found the list on the whole very reliable. And an excellent rule suggested by the authorities in 1965 could surely be copied with advantage in other countries: that all Italian hotel prices should be comprehensive, to include taxes and service charges of every kind, making it much easier for the stranger to calculate costs. What is not always immediately realised is that the rule applies to meals served in hotels to

24

guests not staying there. I learned this the hard way, elsewhere.

Mario Guastoni, owner of the Hotel Margherita, came to greet us. He also manages it, having learned his business in London at the Savoy Hotel in 1952, there again from 1958 and '59, and in between in France and Germany as well as Italy. With a private beach, the Margherita seemed excellent, spotless, many rooms with private bath or shower, all with running hot and cold water that really did run, thanks to an already extensive underground storage system being added to at the time of our visit.

Luncheon, chosen from the ordinary menu, was good, served with care by waiters who like to make a dish look nice and hope you will enjoy it. '*Buon appetito*' is the customary Sardinian courtesy as the plate is set in front of an hotel or restaurant guest.

Earlier, Mario Guastoni had been one of the first managers at the Cala di Volpe, the original hotel to be built by the Aga Khan's *Consorcio*, and so far the only one in Sardinia to be designated as 'Luxury'. The inevitable teething troubles of getting such a new and very sophisticated establishment into its stride would have been considerable in a modern town at any time. In that wild, bare countryside with the then indifferent roads and worse telephone services it must have been a mixture of exasperation and near hysteria. There were yachts wanting supplies, too. 'They wanted ice, and there wasn't any to spare. They wanted fish and fresh fruit, there were only rocks and goats. I tried to run a service using my own car. We sent to Olbia and made the fishmongers open up at two o'clock in the afternoon, but the ice was almost melted and the fish were half cooked by the time we got back'. But somehow it all got into its proper rhythm.

Returning to Olbia we decided to watch the world go by in the evening parade, one of the events of any day in Sard towns or villages whatever the size, as in other Latin countries. Olbia is no exception.

Here, the *piazza* leads off the main street, the Corso, at the top of the hill, and in itself has no particular merit. Three sides are bounded by the usual multiplicity of cafés, bars and barbers' shops, with a few other interests thrown in between. But it is the town meeting place, and thither, to sit at tables under umbrellas come, first, the older men, some with their womenfolk, presently to be joined sometimes by younger, married members of the family. They take their coffee, or drink, or ice-cream, exchange news and gossip, but a little later it is the youngsters who provide the real spectacle, thronging the Corso, disrupting wheeled traffic in the narrow street. Spruced up after the day's work in shops or offices, they look as fresh as paint, as neat as new pins as they saunter along in separate small groups of youths and girls, the latter arm in arm. Up and down they go, just so far in this direction or that, always returning to and from the same point, watching each other out of the corners of observant eyes though feigning an air of complete detachment that doesn't deceive anybody. Occasionally greetings are passed between the sexes, very nonchalantly, sometimes an audible comment intended for passing ears causes a laugh or toss of the head. In fact both sides of this preliminary mating game are acutely aware of each other. After about an hour suddenly the whole scene dissolves, the play is finished.

The girls are small-boned, often with the beautiful carriage inherited from generations of ancestors who carried their burdens on their heads, and their high-pitched chattering, as well as the stronger tones of the young men, had a gay and confident air. The young unmarried girls wore short hair and knee-length skirts, it was only the occasional countrywoman, marketing for the day, who wore the long, swinging skirt and head shawl.

Halfway down the Corso, in the same doorways I had seen them three years previously, sat two tiny women on low stools selling peanuts in pathetically small packets. Chatting with passers-by they seemed to know all and sundry, and doubtless were aware of more of what was going on under the surface than many others of the townspeople. One had obviously in her youth been a beauty, with the straight nose and clear jaw line of almost classic features. Now, the worn, sallow little face was framed in the black shawl round her head, only a wisp of grey hair showing, and she wore the shapeless black garment of older women and widows. I stopped to speak with her and to my astonishment she remembered me, with that sudden brilliant smile that in Sardinia sometimes flashes out. Her whole face lit up, the astonishing vividness of eyes I had not realized were so black an indication of the spirit still there. By and large and with reason, *Sardi* expressions are grave in repose, their look is direct, questioning, and this brief, flashing smile that lights a proud, sombre face is worth seeing, a clue to an inner force.

Leaving Olbia for the Punta Sardegna and the islands Anne Bassett wanted me to see the route through the village of San Panteleo, so off we set, and it was certainly worth the detour. On the edge of the Limbara mountains the road winds in and out, up and down, never to great heights, a *strada bianca* between ragged grey peaks often worn by wind and rain to fantastic shapes, sometimes almost nightmarish in quality. Empty, forbidding, it is a land of tumbled granite and short, dry scrub, the tang of cistus in the air. Under the brilliant blue sky and racing clouds of that day, with the wind in one's face straight off the sea, it had tremendous exhilaration, but could, I thought, on some stormy day have a different, more sinister aspect. A tiny shepherd's hut of stone, tucked among the beetling crags, looked solitary and frail in an odd, helpless way amid such strength.

Eventually the road links up with the main thoroughfare to Palau through Arzachena, and thence to Santa Teresa, the most northerly point of Sardinia, from whose rocks, according to Tyndale, granite was taken for the columns of the Forum in Rome.

When I had last been there, three years previously, the Punta Sardegna and Porto Rafael were wildernesses of rock set in a tangled web of cistus, myrtle, arbutus and similar bushes. Now, Porto Rafael is a sophisticated *piazza* surrounded on three sides by white-painted villas and flats bedded into the native rock in an irregular, pleasing pattern on the hillside. In 1963 the only house was Rafael Neville's, a bungalow painted Roman red, then let to Roddy Wilson the engineer who had superintended the metamorphosis. At that time Rafael, originally the lynch-

pin of the whole idea, lived mostly on his boat, a somewhat
Heath Robinson affair, a converted barge with mod. cons. rather
less than more, and elegant linen covers on the bunks. Trips in
the boat either round the point to the village of Palau, or across
the bay to La Maddelena, always had that pleasant element of
slight uncertainty. It was never quite definite that we would
make port, and once the barge did sink, slowly, fortunately
almost in the harbour of La Maddelena, amid tremendous excitement and noise, fishermen and other friends pushing out in
their boats to the rescue. But for the most part it gave yeoman
service, and I for one was very happy and grateful to be ferried
here and there by this means.

In those days, too, the water supply was a bit haphazard,
mostly carried in a small bore plastic garden hose resting precariously on stones and thorny briars, or at least that was the
result when someone tripped over it. The hose was known to
melt in the sun occasionally, or otherwise spring leaks, and constituted a major headache, though fortunately the actual water,
from an underground river, the Sarrau, now properly piped to
the villas, is very pure.

The original financier of the scheme, who still has an interest
in the land, was the Italian merchant banker in London, Dino
da Ponte, whose plans were publicised with panache by his then
agent, Billy Hamilton, but actual development was eventually
taken over by Roddy Wilson and a partner, Peter Ward. Roddy,
over six feet tall, was full of well controlled Irish charm, but
those bright blue eyes also suggested very single-minded purpose
that was put to good effect in building this village from scratch.
A mechanical engineer whose early training was at the Rolls
Royce works at Derby, and with later experience in development projects in the West Indies, Roddy put first things first,
with the result that pipe lines, electricity and telephone cables
are underground, the drainage system is properly installed, and
water continues to come out of taps, hot and cold. Only electricity and telephone services are sometimes the unhappy victims of local idiosyncracies.

The inlet where Rafael's boat was once tied up in a marshy

bay threaded with blackberry bushes and other hazards was filled in with 350 truck loads of rubble, and is now the *piazza*. The contractor also offered the contents of a cemetery he was clearing but Roddy thought he had better say no to that.

Since St. Patrick's Day 1964 some 30 houses have been built, some of the earliest designed by Michele Busiri Vici, using local labour that not only had to be trained, but whose local prejudices had to be considered. Sards as well as mainland Italians are talented and full of ideas, but reliable construction is not always a strong point, and determined to marry the best of local skill with British thoroughness Roddy gradually carried his masons and electricians along, bearing in mind that islanders, like others of their kind, are very conventional. In Sardinia, the twin expressions *brutta figura*, and *bella figura*, mean much more than putting a bad or a good face on things, they represent a way of life that is serious. When Roddy first explained to his chief mason that he wanted a roof to look as if it was sagging slightly, in order to avoid a stiff, alien look, the man was dumbfounded. 'But I can't do that, all my friends would laugh at me'. This would have suggested *brutta figura* with a vengeance for a craftsman. However, he was presently persuaded, and later brought all his friends along one Sunday to inspect the unbelievable whims of an Irishman. But having agreed to accept such madness the work was well and faithfully done.

All the villas face the sea, and what a vista it is! Northward, across the Straits of Bonifacio, some ten miles away, lies Corsica, rising high out of the water, the mountains plainly visible on a clear day. Much nearer, just across the bay to the north-east is a small archipelago that includes the historic islands of La Maddelena, Caprera and Santo Stefano, the first associated with Nelson, and fleetingly with Mussolini who was held there for a few days in 1943, the second a national monument to Garibaldi, the third the scene of a brief and inglorious episode connected with Napoleon's early career. Between them and the mainland, stretching away into the distance is a sea of unbelievable colour, sometimes blue, sometimes green. The only disadvantage of the Punta Sardegna, if indeed it is a disadvantage, is that there is nearly always a breeze, either blowing off the heights of Corsica, or coming from further eastward, when it is warm and close. But for the most part it is the former, resulting in a freshness that even on the hottest day is wonderfully invigorating.

Sardinia and Corsica are said by geologists and other scientists to be part of the same land mass the rest of which is now sunk in the Mediterranean, to be quite different from either the European continent or from Africa, and the fantastic rock shapes that are such a feature of Gallura are held to be the result of thousands of years of weathering by wind and rain. Nonetheless, in contrary mood, and in face of scientific knowledge, this small island does give to some people exactly the opposite impression, not that only these islands survived, the rest being submerged, but that these were pushed up out of the sea by some enormous upheaval in the distant past, that at one time all these mountains and valleys were swept by the ebb and flow of tremendous currents.

Some of the most astonishing and grotesque rock shapes in the province are on the Punta Sardegna itself, but there are plenty elsewhere in the jagged, tumbled masses of stone, including a weird tortoise near Arzachena, and a famous elephant on the way to Castel Sardo, though the elephant's trunk, poor thing, is beginning to look a bit fragile.

At Porto Rafael the village has become exceedingly international; there are now Austrians, a Pole with a Swedish wife, some French, an American, assorted British, and Italians, one of these last in particular whose purchase of a villa was greeted with some hilarity. He happens to be the charming and very able lawyer to the *Costa Smeralda Consorcio*, who, if rumours were true, were not a little shocked at such defection.

And there is Rafael, the Spaniard, ensconced in a flat above the club which he owns. Outside hang a Spanish and an Italian flag, on the wall is a plaque engraved *Municipio Rafael*. Without him the Punta Sardegna would be a duller place. And he was, after all, the first foreigner in modern times to intrude into this wild, magic coast. His father is a well known Spanish playwright and artist, the head of an ancient and titled family, but inevitably the conventional life of his kind expected of Rafael as the elder son would not be tolerable. So, with the blessing of at least a devoted grandmother who has remained his ever-present help in trouble, Rafael had taken himself further afield, the non-conforming character sometimes met with in one country or another who seems to know and to be known to 'everybody', and to be everybody's friend. Intelligent, cultured, tempera-mental, generous, witty, he tells outrageously funny stories against himself without a quiver in the flat voice, with a completely deadpan expression on the long, pale, melancholy face. Adven-tures in South America as well as Europe included dancing with Josephine Baker, with Katherine Dunham's troupe, also at one time in Paris at the *Folies Bergère*. At this last his performance was completely wrecked one night by seeing his father sitting in the front row. He had come to Paris unannounced to visit his son, found out where Rafael 'worked', and here he was. 'Darling, it was terrible. There was my father, and I was too tall to hide behind anyone else, and I only wore a gold fig leaf. It was such a little leaf.'

I last saw Rafael with a chicken tucked under one arm he had collected from the restaurant for lunch, one of Grazia Deledda's books under the other. Come and share his meal, he suggested, but I was bidden elsewhere and Rafael continued to pick his solitary way on those long legs over the rocky path.

The ferry to La Maddelena plies to and from Palau, some two miles from the Punta Sardegna, and though development in the new village has brought considerable trade there was no outward sign in the rather characterless little fishing village of one long street flanked by small houses and shops that descends to a vague-looking open space hardly worthy of the title of *piazza*. Here are the petrol pumps, here the bus arrives and de-parts for Olbia and other places, belching and shuddering its noisy way after the arrival of the ferry for which it waits. Here, too, is the office where one buys steamer tickets, the quays with a few fishing nets laid out, and at the time of my passing through, from a solitary tramp steamer with a tall mast, cork was being unloaded in a desultory way. On a ledge the old men of the village just sat, with nothing to say, they knew each other too well.

In contrast with the general air of lassitude the Tirrenia company's *traghetto* looked aggressively black and white. There was a general air of vigour aboard. Skyblue corrugated plastic now sheltered the top deck, and just before our departure pop music blared out its message, while a peremptory warning hoot from the bridge brought the usual last minute scramble of latecomers rushing along the jetty laden with insecurely tied packages, with children, and with final messages from friends and relatives being left behind. There were also on this occasion some tearful farewells to a couple of young sailors in spotless white uniforms returning to the naval base at La Maddelena.

The short passage, taking about 20 minutes, is a dangerous one marked by buoys all the way, to which sharp rocks sticking up here and there, and the dark bulk of submerged masses below showing clearly through the water, give emphasis. But there was nothing untoward about this summer day, the water glittered in the sunshine, and under the bright sky gulls soared and swooped on seemingly tireless wings.

La Maddelena is a cheerful little town spreading to right and left as one comes into port, and hitherto the soft pinkish yellow of the old houses with their lovely wrought iron balconies had offered a warm and mellow background to the clusters of fishing boats and other craft at the water's edge, and on the quays to the general assortment of bicycles, cars, people, donkeys, ropes, and the general impedimenta of the sea and seamen. Since my last visit, however, a hideous square block of flats had arisen, thrusting its grey and white chequered bulk above the surrounding buildings like a bad joke. A second sign of modernity as I walked around the quay was the horrid vision of the seven dwarfs in vivid colours, no less, each mannikin about three feet high, now reigning over the portico of the *Ristorante al Mare*, formerly so pleasantly sedate. I dared not venture inside.

The Excelsior had maintained its dismal green, and near by a building in course of erection in 1963 was no further advanced, suffering presumably from the well known complaint of over-enthusiastic planning and insufficient preliminary arithmetic: a trouble also to be met with on the *continente* in the building of hotels as well as private villas.

I was glad to see that the street lighting still had its slightly raffish air, the lamps, two to a standard, each and every one at a different angle and level from all others.

From the mainland, especially at night with the lights flickering across the water, La Maddelena looks larger than it really is, partly due to the fact that it is connected by a causeway with Caprera, and between the town and this latter island the lights of the naval establishment maintain an unbroken link.

Here in 1793 several French warships arrived unexpectedly one night, and a landing was made on the adjacent island of Santo Stefano with the intention of setting up batteries of guns for the bombardment, prior to capture, of La Maddelena. Second in command of a company of artillery was a young Corsican lieutenant, Napoleon Buonaparte, but the islanders repulsed the invading force with such vigour, and returned Napoleon's fire so fiercely, that the French were compelled to retire, and Buonaparte, finding his commanding officer, General Cesari, already departed precipitately, was himself forced to make a hasty evacuation of his position and to leave behind prisoners and stores as well as guns. The occasion is recorded as being the great man's first resounding defeat in war.

Just over ten years afterwards, in October 1803, Nelson arrived with his fleet and anchored in the bay, keeping impatient watch for the French, hoping to engage them emerging from the safety of Toulon harbour. He kept scouts moving in and out among the waters between Sardinia and Southern France until January 1805, when he left suddenly on news that proved inadequate at the time, but still on the long chase that was to end with the annihilation of the French force and his own death off the south of Spain, at Trafalgar, nine months later.

Nelson named these waters 'Agincourt Sound', and his praises of the haven were emphatic and insistent. 'This is one of the finest harbours I have ever seen.' Again and again, with all the urgency he could command, he impressed on Ministers and

c   33

other members of the government, and on anyone else he thought might have influence, the importance of acquiring Sardinia as the British Naval Base in the Mediterranean. If that could be done all the other bases could go hang, and if Britain didn't acquire it the French would surely take it. Tyndale tells of Nelson's efforts with gusto and quotes him at length. To Lord Hobart in December, 1803, Nelson wrote: 'My dear Lord, in presuming to give my opinion on any subject I venture not on infallibility . . . but as my observations on what I see are not unacceptable, I shall state them as they strike me at the moment of writing . . . This, which is the finest island in the Mediterranean, possesses harbours fit for arsenals, and of a capacity to hold our navy within 24 hours sail of Toulon . . . no fleet could pass to the eastward between Sicily and the coast of Barbary, nor through the Faro of Messina . . . ' In another dispatch: 'It is the *summum bonum* of everything which is valuable for us in the Mediterranean. The more I know of it the more I am convinced of its inestimable value, from position, naval port, and resources of all kinds.' But he pleaded in vain.

Nelson was not alone in his opinion. A very different man, John Stuart Mill, is reported to have said that if the British could have Sardinia they would make a garden of the Mediterranean.

Meanwhile, other correspondence and records show Nelson's unremitting preoccupation with the welfare of his ships and their complements, his attention to the smallest detail of stores needed, the type and weight of meat required to be bought, the health of his men. On this last he was enthusiastic. Putting to sea for a cruise he recorded with pride: 'With not one man sick in the Fleet'. And: 'No one dies here, we are the healthiest squadron I ever served in, and all are in good humour.'

This marries with Tyndale's observations that due to the healthy wind there was no *intemperie* on La Maddelena and the rest of the archipelago; that the people here looked so much more lively than their fellows on the Sardinian mainland.

The writer dismissed the somewhat doubtful legend of a liaison between Nelson and a local beauty, Emma Liona, and there is evidence that the former never in fact set foot ashore during the whole fifteen months of his stay, though in those days this was not necessarily any deterrent to the enjoyment of feminine company. That before leaving Nelson presented the local church with a pair of silver candlesticks and a silver crucifix, the pedestal carrying an inscription and engraved with the Brontë arms, has been suggested as a possible *amende honorable* in this connection. But such a gift was not at all unusual following a prolonged stay of a friendly naval or military force, and in view of the fact that the church was comparatively newly built, and probably therefore possessed little plate, this would have made the gesture not only particularly appropriate and acceptable, but very natural as a memento of what appears to have been a pleasant and profitable relationship on both sides. At that period La Maddelena itself was of very recent construction. Prior to the latter end of the eighteenth century it had been very poor, consistently raided by pirates of one sort or another, and almost entirely the resort only of fishermen and of shepherds with flocks of sheep or goats.

And Nelson's health, always frail, was troubling him sorely at this period. Minus an arm and an eye, in frequent pain, he who was always so solicitous of the wellbeing of his fleet could do little to maintain his own. But that the spirit still burned as fiercely as ever is demonstrated in a letter to his brother based on the comment of the French Admiral, Latouche Treville, who, sighting some of Nelson's ships returning to base in Agincourt Sound, following a cruise, boasted that he had 'chased the whole British fleet which had fled before him.' Nelson wrote: 'You will have seen by Latouche's letter how he chased me, and how I ran. I keep it, and if I take him, by God he shall eat it.'

Nelson was something of a fatalist, and certainly gifted with prescience, so it is perhaps permissible to ponder on those famous dying words. Did he really say 'Kiss me, Hardy', or might it rather have been 'Kismet, Hardy'? In *Nelson and his Captains*, W. H. Fitchett describes Nelson's parting with Sir Henry Blackwood on the quarterdeck of the Victory, at the opening of the battle. 'Blackwood expressed the hope that he would greet his Admiral as a victor when the fight was over. "God bless you, Blackwood," said Nelson, "I shall never speak to you again." '

The candlesticks and crucifix are prized possessions in the little church of Santa Maria Maddelena, but I was not able to see them. There was an old woman in the building evidently in charge of some keys, but she was adamant when I asked if I might see the treasures. No, they were not on show, and she didn't know when they would be, she insisted sternly. Coax as I might, and tell her that I was English as was the donor of the gift.

So I decided to have lunch, and unable to find the *trattoria* of a previous visit I went into La Mangana. It was small, scrupulously clean, with green plants in the window, more trained across the ceiling, and there were no flies. At a cost of 12/– I ate grilled fish, salad, a mild cheese, and fresh figs washed down with a local wine, all of which was delicious, and rounded off with the usual tiny cup of good, exceedingly strong black coffee. 'No sugar, thank you', I said, and the *padrone* gazed at me in amazement. 'No sugar, *signora*?' I shook my head. 'No, thank you.' Whereupon he replied gravely, but with a twinkle in his eye: '*Signora*, there is a saying in Sardinia that a lady who takes her coffee bitter (*amaro*) can always be trusted.' I had not heard the expression before but was to meet it again in the province of Nuoro, up in the mountains.

Short of a private car, the best way to go to Caprera is by taxi, the drivers have a definite tariff, and I have always found them patient, helpful and honest. The present occasion was no exception, the driver a handsome young man, full of information and concerned that I should see and learn everything possible. He also constituted himself my camera boy, carrying the heavy case about with the greatest good humour, asking about every piece of equipment, each picture I took. We also went through the usual personal why and wherefore. The Sards are curious and interested in everything concerned with a stranger, particularly a woman travelling alone, but in a frank, uninhibited way that has in it nothing of presumption. Was I alone, why, where had I come from, where was I going to, and so on? The first question was always why was I alone? For Sard women do not travel alone.

My young friend was in some perplexity concerning his own life. Should he join the navy, he asked or try his fortunes in Rome? He had already done his military service. What would I suggest, and when he discovered by dint of question and answer that I was British this touched another avenue of possibility. What about work in England, did he have to have a permit? Was it worthwhile; but it was always foggy and raining in England, wasn't it? At least there was one question I could answer satisfactorily.

The road to Caprera lies through the centre of La Maddelena, past the naval barracks that form an important part of the establishment as a training school for young sailors. On one side the way was lined with feathery purple-tipped tamarisks and huge magnolia trees in full bloom, their heady scent drifting in through the car windows even as we passed. On the other side lies the sea, the island of Santo Stefano, now used for fuel storage, and, tucked against a jetty, three small, grey-painted naval vessels. 'They are old, only used for instruction', I was informed as we dropped down the slope to the causeway set low over the water on a bed of rocks. We went clonkety-clonkety over the loose timbers and then up again, on to the island, the route to the house winding up through aromatic pines, up to the highest point, about 450 feet up.

Lying east and slightly south of La Maddelena, the whole island of Caprera, about five miles at the longest point, and half that width, is now owned by the Italian State, and is preserved as a national monument to Garibaldi, so beautifully described G. M. Trevelyan in *Garibaldi and The Thousand*. '. . . it will, in the rugged grandeur of its scenery and its untouched record of what has been, remain in itself the noblest of all monuments of the Italian Risorgimento . . . Caprera and its white house are seen from a considerable distance out to sea. From the base of the rock precipice that crests the top of the island, the ground on the western side inclines somewhat less steeply to the shore, and where, shining white on the moorside, a quarter of a mile from the water's edge, appears the long, flat-roofed house of one storey, built by Garibaldi and his friends. It is the only object that catches the eye amid grey rocks and dark-green plants that share the island between them. . . . Every cranny in the rock where the earth has lodged, every space between the tumbled boulders, is the cradle of wild vegetation—orchid, lavender, red saxifrage, the stately asphodel, the spurge with its yellow flower, the tamarisk, and the evergreen lentisk with its smooth leaves. But more than all else the cistus, raising its white rock-rose to the traveller's knee . . . indeed, swept as it is by a peculiarly fierce and persistent wind, Caprera has in it more than a touch of the feeling of our northern landscape . . . such an island is not altogether characteristic of Italy, but it is altogether character-istic of Garibaldi.'

To which might perhaps be added that it is, in fact, very characteristic of some other parts of Sardinia.

Setting the complicated scene, the stormy, tragic, triumphant background to this final place of peace, Trevelyan writes: 'On New Year's Day 1859 Italy of the Italians was still confined to the small state of Piedmont, nestling between the Alps and the sea. Strong not in numbers but in the character of its citizens, it enjoyed the respect of Europe, the sympathy of France and England, and the wistful affection of the inhabitants of the other states of the peninsula—sentiments inspired by the well-ordered parliamentary government of King Victor Emmanuel and his Minister, Cavour. The rest of Italy, still partitioned among half a dozen different rulers, was exposed to the absolute power of priests, of foreigners, or of native despots, bound together in a close triple alliance against the rights of the laity, personal free-dom and Italian independence. . . . When, in November 1860, Garibaldi resigned the Dictatorship of Sicily and Naples, and sailed back to his farm on Caprera with a large bag of corn-seed and a small handful of lire notes, he left Victor Emmanuel acknowledged as constitutional monarch in all those territories that we now know as the Kingdom of Italy—with the exception of two or three fortresses where the Bourbon flag flew for yet a few months longer, of the ancient territories of the Venetian Republic, still guarded by the Austrian Quadrilateral, and of that narrow "Patrimony" of the earlier Popes, where the herdsmen and vine-dressers could descry the cupola of St. Peter's floating above the evening mist . . . the Risorgimento movement in Italy herself, after two generations of increasing heat was at boiling point in 1859–60. If the cause had failed again in those years as in 1848–49, it may well be doubted whether these ardours would not have cooled and frozen in despair. . . . If, in short, Cavour, Victor Emmanuel and Garibaldi could not have freed their land in the days of Napoleon III and Palmerston, and while the impulse given by Mazzini was still fresh, it is doubtful whether anyone would have been able to free her at a later period. . . . Garibaldi's great expedition of 1860 carried on the main work of Italian unity, at a time when no other means could have availed for its accomplishment.'

Describing the patriot himself, Trevelyan says: '. . . the qualities which endeared him to the simple souls who lived in his house on Caprera similarly won the hearts of the most critical and experienced judges of men in Italy and England . . . all plainly marked in his port and presence, his voice and his eyes—made him not the greatest, but the unique figure of the age. . . . The story of that auspicious hour when the old-new nation of Italy achieved her deliverance by the wisdom of Cavour and the valour of Garibaldi will remain with mankind to warn the rash that the brave man, whatever he and his friends may think, cannot dispense with the guidance of the wise—and to teach the prudent that in the uncertain currents of the world's affairs, there come rare moments, hard to distinguish but fatal to let slip, when caution is dangerous, when all must be set upon a hazard, and out of the simple man is ordained strength.'

Garibaldi's first visit to the islands, this time to La Maddelena, was in October 1849, as the guest of his friend Francesco Susini during one of those many periods of banishment from Italy, and very shortly after his adored wife, Anita, had died in his arms on the flight from Rome pursued by the Austrians through the marshes of Ravenna. It was not until 1855 that he actually bought the property on Caprera, and from the following year until his death on June 2nd, 1882, this was his home, his refuge, to which he returned always. Nowadays, on that anniversary, there is a procession to his tomb where a wreath is laid, that was at one time attended by the President himself, with his Ministers.

Born on July 4th, 1807, at Nice, then still Italian and known as Nizza, Giuseppe Maria Garibaldi, one of five children born to Domenico Garibaldi and his wife Rosa, was originally intended by his parents for the church, and to this end was sent to a priest to be educated. But this was not the vocation for the lively boy born by the sea and with its restlessness strong in him. Following a brief passage by ship to Genoa he pleaded with his father to let him become a sailor. Now, full circle, it is sailors who have the care of the little house and garden, a young sailor who stands guard always in front of the granite tomb.

Membership in 1833 of Mazzini's recently formed 'Italian Youth' organization resulted almost immediately in the young Garibaldi being condemned to death for his part the following year in an abortive rising organized by the movement. He escaped to America and thus began 20 years of exile and wandering, but years during which his genius for guerrilla warfare was developed and tried in the pampas of South America helping to fight the tyrants and for the independence of the Rio Grande, and of Uruguay. Here he met the beautiful Anita to whom he was married in Montevideo in 1842, and by whom he subsequently had four children—Menotti, Teresita, Rosita and Ricciotti.

Work in a candle factory in New York, long voyages as sailor and subsequently as sea captain to lands as far from his beloved Italy as Australia and the Far East, as well as journeys nearer home, to England, and to North Africa, where the British Consul in Tangier gave him sanctuary for several months, were but interims. Occasional, brief sojourns in Nice where his mother and friends helped to look after his children were for him part of the weariness of waiting for the moment to participate actively once more in the struggle against Austria and other oppressors of his country. After his unavailing efforts in the battles of 1849 he returned to North America via La Maddelena. In New York he met a merchant friend from Genoa and subsequently went to sea again, finally in 1852 as captain of a 1200 ton ship, the Commonwealth, bound for Newcastle, and eventually, Genoa.

He wrote sadly to his friend Vecchi: 'Yes, I am athirst for the emancipation of our country, and you may be sure that this wretched life of mine, though sadly the worse for wear, would be again honourably dedicated to so holy a cause . . . I am terrified at the likely prospect of never again wielding sword or musket for Italy.'

But his time was to come and his patience to be rewarded.

In 1856, however, there was nothing to do but wait. On Caprera with his elder son, Menotti, he set about the task of building, though he himself was not very good at it. But what was done was well enough, some of it with the aid of friends who flocked to the little dwelling and shared the simple living. Garibaldi imported some specially good goats from Malta, and with his gentle affection for animals took the greatest care also of the cows, each of which was known by name. He helped to till the ground, sowed corn and vegetables, made a flower garden, and when depression seized him more deeply than usual he would wander away alone, to the solitude of the rocks, those vivid seas all around him, and the wind.

According to Trevelyan there are traces of pre-Roman habitation on Caprera, but in the centuries immediately preceeding the arrival of Garibaldi the island had only been occupied by a few shepherds and their flocks, and by the descendants of a bandit, Ferraciolo, who soon became friends with the newcomer. Not so, unfortunately, the only other residents, an ill-favoured Englishman named Collins married to a rich and devoted wife whose gentle good humour was a marvel to all who knew them. Collins' livestock and that of Garibaldi trespassed equally, with unhappy results, so presently, in self-defence, Garibaldi built a wall round his property, but in due course was freed from his surly neighbour by Collins' death. Shortly afterwards some English friends together bought the rest of the island for him from the amiable widow who had retired to another house she owned on La Maddelena.

The garden is still laid out as in Garibaldi's day, and in the centre of the main courtyard, its heavy branches supported by stout props, is the now great tree he planted to celebrate the birth of his daughter Clelia in 1867. The last of all his children to survive, she lived to a great age, dying there in her own part of the house only as recently as 1959.

Round the white wall that encircles and shelters the garden, and round the house itself flowers riot—bougainvillia, roses, geraniums, hydrangeas grown to great bushes, gladioli, carnations, and at the side of the house by the olive plantation, violets. The scent of rosemary and thyme mingles with a thousand others, and with that of pine and cistus borne in on the breeze. The small hut where Garibaldi and Menotti lived while first they were building a more suitable habitation for Terasita is tucked into the wall. The dog kennel, the workshop and the laboratory are still intact. Indoors are preserved the simple articles of Garibaldi's daily life, along with many tributes to his valour. His medicines are in a bookcase, there are his writing materials, the red shirt, weapons, the saddle of his horse Marsala, named after the landing with his Thousand, ribbons from the hats of men who had sailed with him. And there is the little carriage in which he was carried round the grounds as his wounds and other ills afflicted him more and more. At the door of the room in which he died, just inside, is the wall clock, that was stopped at the hour of his death. On another wall hangs a calendar of the type having a single page to a day. The yellowing sheet records June 2nd, 1882. In the centre of the room, set as the dying man wished so that his eyes could look their last northward, to the Corsica he so wanted to be joined to Italy, and beyond, to Italy itself, is a small, high fourposter iron bed, the white lace coverlet smoothly laid, the pillows high. A young sailor showing me round touched the pillow gently, as though here had lain a loved and loving father. 'See, this is as it was when he died.'

He bade me come with him to examine the portraits of family

and friends, the framed tributes lining the walls. Among them is a large parchment inscribed in a beautiful copperplate hand from the National Reform League of Adelphi Terrace, Strand, dated May 9th, 1867. It is signed 'Beales, President', and is addressed to: 'Italy's Honoured Patriot and London's Illustrious Citizen, General Garibaldi' in token of acceptance of the Honorary Presidency of the League. Part of the inscription reads: '... the strength and prosperity of a Nation is to be found in the Unity and Harmony of all classes under a Government dependent upon the free choice of the people and administration of public affairs in accordance with the will and for the interests of the people.'

In the very simplicity of the house and manner of preservation of the memorial, and the tranquil silence that surrounds it, is a great serenity. In the garden, a path leading gently downwards takes the visitor to where are the tombs of Garibaldi, his third wife Francesca and other members of the family including an illegitimate daughter Anita, who died in 1875 at the age of 16.

That Garibaldi was devoted to his first wife, whose heroism and death shattered him for a time, is undenied. That, subsequently, he had a roving eye for the opposite sex is apparent also. Trevelyan reports that during 1855, when he spent some months at Nice with his mother and his children, 'the evenings he spent at a house rented by an English widow lady to whom he was for a time engaged'. Later, a liaison with Battistina Ravella is recorded officially, with the bland statement: '*non sposata*', and it was of this union that Anita was born, to die so young. A year later he somewhat rashly married the handsome young Contessa Raimondi who had courageously brought news of the Austrian dispositions to him across the mountains during the Alpine campaign. Garibaldi was then 52 years old and the union, such as it was, ended on the wedding day, as dramatically as it had begun. According to Trevelyan: 'On January 24th, 1860, the ceremony took place at Fino, but before nightfall a letter was put into his hand which proved that she was in the habit of favouring a younger man. Full of "bad thoughts", but "terribly cool in his demeanour" he sought through the house till he came to his wife's room, and asked her if she had written the letter. She confessed it. "Then see", he said, "that you do not bear my name; I leave you for ever." '

The marriage was annulled, but not until January 14th, 1880, and less than a fortnight later he married Francesca Armosino who had already borne him three children, Clelia, Rosita, and Manlio, who cared for him devotedly until his death, and at his specific request was eventually buried beside him.

In the grounds, on a rounded rock, is the bakehouse where the bread for the household was made, and close by, on a slightly higher eminence, stands a large bust of Garibaldi, placed so that the beautifully carved head faces north. It is at once moving and powerful, gnarled hands holding his shawl close, the sadness that invests the thoughtful face masterly and haunting. From that spot the view across the island, over the blue sea, is glorious, the only addition to Trevelyan's description an encampment down by the shore of a group of Club Méditerranée huts, but their shape and colour draw them into the natural tawny background of cistus and dried herbage, their distance giving a slightly unreal impression as part of a backcloth.

Part Two
*
SASSARI

For administrative purposes Sardinia is divided into three provinces, Cagliari, Nuoro and Sassari, this last stretching right across the northern part of the island, with Gallura as the largest region. Tempio is the capital of Gallura, seat of a bishop and centre of the long-established cork industry. Returning to Sassari, with my early dilemma in mind on the subject of the route, I decided to take the main road through Tempio, in any case it is a very beautiful one.

On this morning a reluctant sun came and went fitfully, big grey clouds banking up presently to hide it completely. Almost as far as the Tempio-Aggius junction the route is comparatively straight, that is, straight for Sardinia, where the roads have more hairpin bends to the mile than almost any I know. But not to spoil the record, this one wriggles in the neighbourhood of Santa Maria di Neve, growing greener and greener, steeper and steeper, always with that magnificent sweep of mountain and valley so typical of the entire island, and marking the difference with many other mountainous regions. In this generous, bold land only very rarely are valleys shut in, tight, claustrophobic.

Rain was threatening, some had already fallen earlier accentuating in the clear air the scent of roadside flowers, one of the marvels of this drive in spring and early summer. Here were poppies, honeysuckle, scabias, vetch, yellow toadflax, violets, and a brilliant sky-blue flower on a tough branching stalk whose name I never did discover. There were several variations of cow parsley, single spikes of thistle raised proud coronets of purple, along the ground a soft carpet of a creeping plant with tiny pink and white flowers among a rainbow-hued mass of other blossom

45

that at once enchanted and made me ashamed of my botanical ignorance. Above these lovely, wild herbaceous borders were blackberries in such clusters as I had never previously seen. Around them hung the soft humming of bees. Here, too, the rock rose still spread its white stars unlike the cistus in the more exposed coastal districts which had done with flowering and was already, at the beginning of June, filling the air with its resinous tang.

Here were thyme and rosemary as well, to add fragrance to the scented air; then, as the road progressed, more and more cork trees, gnarled and some reputed to be several hundred years old. They covered the rising foothills of the mountains, stripped of the valuable bark to a height of eight or nine feet, the vivid copper-coloured, smooth inner fibre of the trunk looking slightly comic and undressed beneath the severe dark foliage above. The bark is taken away on an average every ninth year, and with it comes a thin layer of the tawny fibrous tissue that clings to the outer layer of cork. This, peeled from the bark, is the *camisia*—the shirt—that with other herbs has for centuries been used to dye the crisp dark, red-brown cloth, a mixture of wool and goat hair, used by the women for the long pleated skirts of their traditional costumes, as well as for garments for their menfolk.

Though not quite 2,000 feet up, nearing Tempio the air grows cooler. Only a short distance from the highest peak of the Limbara range, the Punta Balestieri, 4,590 feet high, and often snow covered from November to April, the town and immediate vicinity have an enviable reputation for healthiness by virtue of proximity to the crisp, invigorating mountain breezes. Tyndale refers to the Tempiese as being strong, athletic and healthy, as well as shrewd and clever, in contrast with the inhabitants of lower lands. In the area are the thermal springs of Rimaggiu and the rivers flowing down from the heights fed by winter snow, produce sufficient water for Tempio to have been used as a source of supply for the *Costa Smeralda*, to which tankers were sent daily until a properly piped local service had been established.

The town itself has a somewhat grey and faded air, possibly deceptive, particularly for the traveller there only briefly, because in Sardinian villages and small towns such as this doors and windows of houses are kept shut—though not often locked —and even small shops are anonymous without names over them, individual identity hidden behind the dense curtains of plastic fringe that keep out flies. And except in the few cities and larger towns it is rare to see a garden from the road. Not that they aren't there, indeed they are, but either Arab style, in a courtyard inside the open square of the house, or in any case, behind tall closed gates set in equally tall walls. Again and again, the sudden opening of such gates revealed a beautifully kept little garden, a riot of lovely flowers. This is not intended as a demonstration against mere theft, or spoilation, the Sards are basically an honest and dignified people, but it is an interesting facet of a perilous life behind stockades that was once everyday fact.

In Tempio is to be seen a variation of the Sardinian skill in wrought iron work, generally most obvious in the form of beautifully fashioned balconies everywhere. Here, it is particularly shown in fanlights over narrow doors, the semicircles of ironwork in designs either incorporating initials, or sometimes signs such as Aaron's rod, with entwined snakes, making one wonder whether this particular one was originally, or perhaps even then, the doctor's house.

This is an area of animal transport, of bullock carts, horses and donkeys, though, unexpectedly, I never saw a mule in the whole of the island. The Sard is by tradition proud of his horse, which in medieval days was the subject of protective laws, and whenever I saw any, which was frequently in some districts, they were always in good condition, with none of that neglected, frightened air so often unhappily obvious on the *continente*. Just north of Barumini, in the plain of Gesturi, there are still some wild horses that are carefully protected. As the tilled land, the olive gardens, cork plantations and vineyards demonstrate patient, careful husbandry, so, too, bullocks and other cattle, as well as horses and donkeys, reflected pride of possession.

47

The *Tempiese* and people of the surrounding countryside are noted for their songs, and at *festas* for their skill in extemporising, adding topical verses almost in the manner of calypsos to traditional pieces. If a stranger is present on such an occasion he—or she—will certainly be included and asked to contribute. Gavino Pes, one of the island's most renowned poets was born here, and Aggius, visible on its peak across a green valley, had a choir which won international acclaim and took part in a Welsh Eisteddfod.

Less peaceful than song making is the history of Aggius in relation to a *vendetta alla morte* which, starting from the covetous eyes of a married man having been cast on a forbidden daughter, resulted over the years that followed in 72 assassinations, leaving only six survivors between the two families before peace was established.

From Tempio to Sassari the road continues twisting and turning, up and down, vineyards presently taking the place to some extent of cork forests, and more olive groves through Perfugas and Nulvi, the latter with a forlorn desolate air not at all dispelled by the sight of the older women of the village, obviously of a malarial generation, many stooped, with a sad, worn look in their eyes, as if they had given all their strength in the production of the next generation and now, as only the *Nonne*, the grandmothers, were of little value. Livening the scene, however, were the children, darting this way and that, returning home after morning school, the younger ones like little gnomes, clad in black overalls with soft white collars tied with bright red ribbons, some of the small girls with matching bows on the tops of their young heads. They seemed lively enough.

By the time I reached Osilo, high upon its hill by a fifteenth-century fortress, it was raining hard, the air heavy, close. More and more vines, olives and now, also, fig trees took the eye, surrounded by prickly pear hedges, beautifully contained, the pale, fragile flowers looking totally unreal stuck on the tips of the thick, fleshy spikes. And here began the more frequent roadside decoration of oleanders that, from now on, garlanded highways, foothills and villages in every shade from white through pinks

Porto Rafael

Rocks on the Punta Sardegna

Caprera—the statue of Garibaldi

On the road to Dorgali with Monte Oliena in the background

Castel Sardo

to deep bluish reds, and in southern Sardinia particularly, including the soft pinkish-yellow tone of the ripe apricot.

The main streets of Sassari abound with flowering trees and shrubs, looking and smelling fresh and lovely in the rain as I pulled up alongside the kerb to enquire of a couple of *carabinieri* just coming out of a gate the whereabouts of the Tourist office. Said one, a heavily built man with a pleasant, placid face: '*Signora*, if I may I will come with you and show you. There are rather a lot of one-way streets that are difficult for a stranger, and I am going in that direction.' What could be better? In he got, and in no time at all we were in the Piazza d'Italia, outside the Palazzo Giordano, a nineteenth-century building and, as luck would have it, in an empty parking space immediately in front of the big double doors.

The second largest city in Sardinia, rival of Cagliari, the capital, in the south, Sassari gives the impression of having a very proper sense of its importance as the busy commercial centre of the north. Also of having had an Italian President as one of its citizens—President Segni was born there.

With a population now of nearly 100,000, it is built on hilly ground at an altitude of some 700 feet, the new part of the city with its big blocks of flats and colonnaded shops mostly giving off wide tree and oleander-lined avenues to the north and west, up from the Piazza d'Italia; while below the adjacent, older Piazza Cavallino, more ancient, narrow streets wind down and about in the vicinity of the cathedral and the market.

Sassari owed its importance in the beginning to the tribulations of the Roman port of Turris Libissonis—now Porto Torres —whose citizens, after repeated invasions by Vandals, Saracens and other enemies, and eventually the sack of the town by the Genoese in 1166, retreated ten miles inland to the south, to the then little village of Sassari. Though that was not the end of their troubles, for Sassari in its turn became for several hundred years the scene of strife between *Aragonesi*, *Pisani* and *Genovesi*, with eventual victory to the last mentioned in the late fourteenth century. And it is the Genoese influence that is most to be seen

D

in the older parts of the city and that probably remains in the blood of many of the citizens of modern Sassari.

Rivalry with Cagliari was—and is—not the only jealousy. Tyndale relates that feeling between Alghero and Sassari became so acute at one time that citizens from Sassari entering the former town were required to take their swords from their scabbards and leave them at the gate on arrival. Against which the *Sassaresi* retaliated by making the *Algheresi* not only leave their swords on entry, they were ridiculed by being obliged to wear an additional empty scabbard, one on the right as well as the left. Though such visible signs are no longer to be seen, officials in Sassari are certainly very conscious of civic pride. 'We are autonomous here', was a remark I heard more than once.

The Palazzo Giordano is shared with a bank, the tourist organization's offices being on the first floor. I had spoken with the Director, Doctor Mura, the previous day from Porto Rafael, after much time and patience required to get a number no more than 60 miles away, and had promised to try to arrive just before luncheon, one o'clock. Now it was five minutes past the hour, the place was shut and locked, the rain pelting down, I was clad only in a cotton blouse and skirt, with espadrilles on my feet. And what was really important at this moment, I didn't know at which hotel I was supposed to be staying. Stupidly enough I hadn't ascertained this in advance, the booking having been kindly made for me by the *Turismo*.

Surveying the immediate situation somewhat pessimistically I remembered a café, the Mokador, where I had once had a quick and good hot meal with Rafael, on a slightly hysterical and unreal trip from the Punta Sardegna to Alghero that was to have started at 9 a.m. 'No later, Mary, promise. I've got so much to do.' I promised. In fact Rafael finally collected himself and all that was necessary somewhere about 3 p.m., and with various stops on the way, including Tempio and Sassari, where we had a much needed meal, we eventually arrived at our destination at some unrealised hour after midnight. The whole venture was rounded off about 3 a. m. when my bed, literally, collapsed. The springs subsided with a horrid, unmusical twang

to the ground, complete with me. I had been sound asleep, but
the only thing to do at that hour was to pull mattress and bed-
clothes clear of the wreckage and continue the night on the floor.
Which I did.

So, for the second time in quiet distress, I repaired to the
Mokador and had an excellent lunch of roast veal, vegetables,
fruit, a glass of wine and an excellent cup of coffee for about ten
shillings. It is a place much patronised by office and other
workers, as well as by country people in Sassari for the day, and
hot dishes as well as cold are first class. Great pans of freshly
cooked meats, of pasta, fish and other foods are kept hot over
steam heat, portions are ample. Watching the comings and
goings rather than the leaden skies I prolonged my meal as far
as I decently could, finally taking a long time to eat some
delicious cherries, and to drink my coffee.

After a time the rain more or less ceased and I returned to
the car. About 3.30 I observed that a little shop selling tourist
goods, tucked into a corner of the *piazza*, was opening again. I
asked the girl in charge when the *Turismo* office would be func-
tioning again, too. Oh, not in the afternoon at all, she thought.
That, however, was a prospect I was not yet prepared to accept,
so presently I mounted the marble steps once more. Sards
always come to the rescue of a stranger, and a man going to the
bank offices on the same floor enquired if I was in trouble, could
he help? I explained my difficulty and forthwith he led me to a
small, side door and beat a tattoo, as well as finding a micro-
scopic bell which he pressed firmly. This brought a quiet man
to open the door at last. All indignation on my behalf, my kind
friend said the *signora* had been waiting literally hours, she was
a stranger, it was disgraceful, what did they propose to do about
it.

I was invited in with the greatest courtesy, and regret that
there had perhaps been some misunderstanding. But no, Doctor
Mura was not yet here, and it transpired that in his absence
nothing could be done. No, they were not sure about the hotel,
they thought accommodation had been booked at the Jolly but,
there were two of that name, and one would have to await the

return of *Il Direttore*. As I knew from past experience elsewhere, decentralization is not, unfortunately, a habit of Italian official organizations, so there was nothing to do but wait.

Dr Mura arrived at 6.30 as I was about to leave. Small, spare, grey haired and bespectacled, he had been in the service of the *Turismo* for 27 years and was a mine of information. Obviously, he also had very definite opinions as to the position of women in the state of things; a family man himself with an eldest son of nearly 30, the youngest of his children not yet 10, he told me severely: 'We do not have women working here. In Italy girls in offices are not very intelligent, and in any case nobody does any work, the girls are always showing off and the men preen themselves, forgetting about the job.' However, we discussed places of especial interest, and Dr Mura was good enough to agree to provide me with a driver for my car who knew the roads, which would certainly be a help. 'He is a good lad', said the Director. Luigi, the 'good lad', turned out to be a placid, solidly built man in his early thirties who presently piloted me to the Grazia Deledda Jolly in the viale Dante, and promised to return at 9 a.m. the next morning to take me to Castel Sardo.

The Grazia Deledda hotel, named after the famous Sard authoress, is the newer and larger of the two Jolly hotels in Sassari, one of six in Sardinia, and of the chain now to be found throughout the mainland of Italy, and in Sicily. To know one Jolly is to know them all, a deliberate policy, partly intended as a recognisable certificate of quality, and partly, presumably, as a means of keeping down prices in terms of equipment. The organization was started by a northern Italian industrialist who, travelling in southern Italy on business some years ago, discovered the then almost total lack of hotels where travellers wishing to stay for limited periods could find reasonable accommodation and efficiency. Most of the Jollys are graded as first class, many have air conditioning, furnishings are almost identical, simple but adequate, the beds comfortable, there are private bathrooms or showers, the food is limited in terms of choice, but otherwise good, all those in which I have stayed both on the mainland and in Sardinia are extremely clean, the service is good and pleasant. If menus tend to be limited 'international Italian' rather than including local specialities, that also has to do with central buying and therefore economy, the endeavour being to keep prices down as far as possible. There is no Signor Jolly, as I have heard suggested. The name is a colloquialism for the Joker in a pack of cards, the inference being that if you have the Joker you have all you need.

The Grazia Deledda was no exception to the general rule and I was soon installed in a comfortable room on the fourth floor looking westward over the city in the golden light of the setting sun.

Presently I took my way down to the restaurant. As with many of the newer Jollys the kitchen here was separated from the dining room only by a huge plate glass window, behind which the chef in the tallest and whitest of hats was busily engaged with members of his *brigade*. Clients were apparently a cross section of town and country people, mostly men, and all eyes swivelled instantly when in walked an obvious model girl in a trouser suit, followed by an older woman and a man. With the not unusual bony, vacuous face of her kind, partly obscured by short, straight hair, the lanky, beanpole girl ran the gauntlet of those curious eyes with conspicuous ease, but once the party was installed in their corner they were quickly forgotten. Obviously the girl was merely a spectacle rather than an attraction, the magnetism wasn't there.

In contrast, another girl coming in later immediately took, and held, all eyes. She was quite lovely and knew it. Shining red-gold hair was swept up from the delicately boned oval face and held at the back of her head by a ribbon bow. A high-necked, sleeveless dress of a soft silk print in shades of blue and green complemented the fair skin and beautiful column of her throat; her only jewels the flashing diamond and a wedding ring on the slim, manicured hand with its rosy fingertips that lay so lightly on the white cloth, establishing her status instantly. As she took her seat at a table, with a gay and devastating smile, the young waiters nearly fell over each other to get there first. And from then on it was a delicious comedy of manners played with fascinating grace and perfect propriety on both sides, and utterly Italian. When she left the whole *ambiente* changed, to fall with a dull thud into the mundane business of setting tables and carrying food.

The next morning, the rain no more, Luigi and I set out for Castel Sardo via Sennori and Sorso under a brilliant sky, along a route through olive groves and fruit orchards, some bordered by the lovely, old dry stone walls, others by perfectly contained hedges of prickly pear now tipped with delicate yellow blossoms. How the *Sardi* manage it I do not know, but again and again there was this marvellous precision of prickly pear barriers completely regular and straight, and one would think very effective in repelling intruders of any kind, two- or four-legged. But the work involved must be very skilled, and hard. In other Mediterranean countries the prickly pear is a menace. Not in Sardinia, as far as one could see.

Here, again, roadsides were bedecked with oleanders, as well as with broom, acacias and tamarisks in between the flickering leaves of tall poplars and eucalyptus trees; beneath, a carpet of flowers almost as lovely as that on the Tempio road. Presently the silver of olives gave way to the bright, pale green of vines, low and neat, which provide the grapes for the local Cannonau wine. Here and there fields of purple artichokes were being allowed to go to seed, the air was full of the sounds of small birds, and the light was softer than might have been thought possible consonant with such brilliant sunshine.

As the winding road over the rolling hills dropped to the coast, miles of empty, white sandy beaches came into view, a lazy, translucent turquoise sea just curling at the edges of the shore the road running alongside. In the distance the ancient fortress of Castel Sardo stood high on its promontory over the water.

Built by the Genoese Doria family in the twelfth century, originally known as *Castel Genovese* but renamed by Carlo Emmanuele III in the eighteenth century, the medieval castle once had a dominating and important role in the region on this north-eastern tip of the Gulf of Asinara. Now decaying, battlements loom over the newer village gradually taking shape down

below, a seemingly incongruous marriage of style, though doubtless for the owners of the modern, square houses with their
rose-red roofs and sometimes rakish air created by unexpectedly
mauve, green or blue chimneys, more physically comfortable
than the dwellings in the warren opening either side of the cobbled way that meanders to the summit, where a *carabinieri* post
is now established.

Apart from lobster fishing which engages the men, an important, long-established industry of basket making is the occupation of almost every female from small girls to their grandmothers. Made from local dwarf palms it is skilled, traditional
work, individual families often using particular emblems of red,
green or black, or sometimes all three as decoration. This is fine
craftsmanship and though it is on sale throughout Sardinia, and
also made elsewhere, Castel Sardo is the centre for this type.
And with wares of several kinds, including the coarser but
equally skilled baskets and trays made from the asphodel lily,
is on sale here, together with some of the beautiful hand woven
rugs from Dorgali, and, inevitably, postcards.

Halfway up the climb the road splits, creating the nearest
thing to a *piazza*, and here, on a stone ledge were sitting the old
men of the community like a row of grey sparrows. Gnarled
hands on sticks, rheumy eyes gazing it often seems at nothing,
knowing each other too long and too well perhaps for there to be
anything left of conversation, they perch on sheltered ledges in
villages and towns, but especially in villages, all over the island,
as much a part of Sardinian life as the *macchia*.

We struggled, panting, at least I was panting, to the top, to
a wide view northwards across the sea to Corsica, a faint blue
smudge on the horizon; south and east to blue-shadowed mountains, and west, across the bay, to Capo Falcone and the island
of Asinara, and in the near distance, beyond the chocolate earth,
to the neat husbandry of the olive groves and vineyards through
which we had come.

Nearly at the top of the *castello*, from a niche in the rock, came
odd sounds which we investigated, to find two baby falcons,
wide open beaks and fierce round eyes demanding food and

more food. They were the treasure of a boy who had found them fallen from the nest, he said, as he held out a hand quietly, making little clucking noises. The birds were untethered, quite free, and one hopped fearlessly on to the outstretched fingers, still complaining loudly. The mottled plumage of adulthood was just beginning to show through the baby fluff, and the proud young owner announced that he was going to train them for hunting.

*   *   *

Back in Sassari I walked down into the town among the shops below the Piazza Cavallino, looking for a cobbler's and a hairdresser, and needing also to buy a comb for which I went into an elegant, small shop selling famous brands of beauty preparations and similar quality goods. Having bought the comb I sought advice on my other two problems, and forthwith the *padrone* insisted that a lad in his shop should go with me. 'These old streets are complicated' he suggested, with reason. So we set off, the youth waiting while I had my conversation with the cobbler on the subject a minor repair, then escorting me to what turned out to be an excellent hairdresser. Three days later I had occasion to go again to the shop, the *padrone* recognized me instantly, hoped both errands had been to my satisfaction, and appeared delighted at my approval.

Returning to the piazza I sat down outside a café to watch the world go by, shops and offices were closing and the whole of Sassari appeared to be abroad, the occasional countrywoman in her long, dark, pleated skirt and black head shawl in sombre contrast to the short-skirted city girls in their gay, sleeveless summer dresses. But there was in the proud carriage of the countrywomen, in their often worn faces a dignity and courage that matched their splendid bearing and free stride. Baby Fiat cars buzzed around the square like hurrying beetles, and motor scooters were almost wheel to wheel, travelling at an apparently alarming rate. In fact the traffic was very well organized, a noticeable condition throughout the whole island. Accidents there are, especially on the outskirts of Cagliari, but covering more than 4,000 kilometres I never saw one, whereas in Calabria the year previously I had seen one almost every day.

The road police, sometimes confused by visitors with other police, appear to do a very good job checking the efficiency of vehicles, their presence a warning not to overstep the mark. Apart from questions of speed and the prevention of other obvious faults, they have authority to make spot checks of lights, brakes and similar essentials, and to stop vehicles carrying too many passengers, as well as inspecting licences. In the event of difficulty on an isloated road they can be very helpful. I was stopped only once, near Dorgali. 'Have you got your red triangle?' I was asked, my blank stare betraying utter forgetfulness of a regulation. One of the policemen moved towards the front of the car—it was a Fiat 850 with a rear engine— I flicked over the switch and he opened the bonnet to find, to my relief, the article in question. It folds into quite a small space and I had overlooked its existence completely. The law requires it to be set in the road 30 yards behind a vehicle which may be stationary from any cause. My lapse was excused on this occasion with an admonitory wave of a finger, and I was sped on my way with a smart salute, a smile, and the injunction not to forget to use the triangle should the need arise, which, gallantly, they hoped it would not.

Behind the Piazza Cavallino in Sassari narrow streets wind down to the cathedral, a fourteenth-century building much added to over the centuries, with an ornate seventeenth-century façade in the Spanish baroque style, of which the *Sassaresi* are very proud. Surrounding it are old houses with traces of eighteenth-century and earlier elegance in doorways and windows, and what was obviously once a beautiful *palazzo*, all together now a jumble of poorer and decaying buildings which seems very sad. Still lower down the hill, near the market, is the Rosello fountain, carved with four statues representing the four seasons; built in 1605 it is said to be fed from an underground stream that never runs dry.

The large Piazza d'Italia is the centre of *Sassaresi* life, the Trafalgar Square of the city, where every evening half the population takes its evening stroll. In the centre a marble statue of Vittorio Emmanuele II surrounded by four palm trees gazes rather severely from under the brim of a plumed hat on top of which irreverent pigeons are usually perched. Round the statue children race, others feed the pigeons, their elders chatting, or just standing. On the far side is the eighteenth-century Ducal Palace, a graceful building of pale stone, now the Town Hall, and from it a wide modern thoroughfare, the via Roma, leads towards the Museum; behind it, the viale Umberto eventually gives on to the Municipal sports ground. The via Roma offers an interesting sidelight on local life. On one side is a colonnade, with a few shops, several cafés, and bookstalls; here the older men gather. On the opposite side of the road, higher up, is another café, the meeting place of the younger generation, and as far as I could see, never the twain did meet.

Facing the latter, on the corner of the via Deffenu, a great wall rises, enclosing a large island site. As I walked back to the Jolly I gazed up at this enormous barrier, and the reason for it then became apparent. It was the prison. On what was obviously a catwalk just inside the top of the wall sentries armed with automatic rifles paced backwards and forwards in ceaseless patrol. In the centre, three large blocks reared stark masses above even the wall, small barred windows proclaiming their occupation. Originally the gaol had been on the outskirts of the city, now modern development had caught up with and passed it. Once or twice bearded faces pressed close to the bars were visible, and I wondered whether the noise and bustle of a busy city all round was an aggravation or the opposite. In the summer sunshine it made one's own limited freedom so much greater by comparison. Each time I went by I noticed swallows wheeling and swooping over the heart of the enclosure, never over surrounding buildings, and I wondered why.

The next day promised glorious weather, not a cloud was to be seen. But Luigi seemed depressed when he came to collect me. After a while it emerged that family cares were weighing somewhat. He had two small daughters of 4 and 2, just that, daughters! This was the trouble. Well, I suggested, endeavouring to be comforting, perhaps you will now have two sons and that will make a very good family, the girls will help to look after the boys. But Luigi shook a lugubrious head. Two girls were enough; if a third child should be another girl that would be altogether too much. I saw that three girls in a row would certainly be a case of *brutta figura* again, so we changed the subject.

Formerly a member of the *carabinieri*, for six years of his service mostly in Rome, Luigi had found the hours too difficult for the maintenance of reasonable family life, so had given up the police job, but had kept an abiding passion for Judo, at which he was already something of an expert, a Black Belt. It was his greatest ambition to achieve a high degree of Dan, an emminence that he reckoned would take at least four or five more years, but which he felt would be worth striving for, particularly if meanwhile he could also merit being chosen to compete in the next Olympics. He was, I understood, already one of the four best exponents of the art in Italy; meanwhile he was going down to Bosa next weekend to give a demonstration. I began to understand why three or more girls in a row might present an unfortunate background. There was a likeable, bulldog quality about this not over-intelligent man, and I had already noticed that he was astonishingly light and quick on his feet for one of his bulk. One could only hope that Judo success would compensate for that lack of sons, and that the imagined reproach to his masculinity would be so balanced.

We were bound for Porto Torres, and beyond it, Stintino and Capo Falcone, but on the way made a detour for Luigi to show me Platamona, the *Marina di Sassari*, a Mecca every summer weekend for thousands of *Sassaresi*. The way led over an open plain soon after leaving the city, through vines and olives to cornfields, and presently, as we came to loose, sandy soil, to more pines and eucalyptus and the most magnificent oleanders I had yet seen. Adjacent to the beach, if so long a stretch of sand can be thus designated, is the Pontinental Hotel, a large, first class *albergo*, much and happily patronised by British group tours.

The beach goes on for miles, at the railed off point of entry a first section being reserved for the *militare* and their families. A long centre portion is the happy playground of lesser folk, and finally come the private lock-up cabins, four deep, shady parking lots, umbrellas, chairs and all the rest of the paraphernalia for those who take their recreation more luxuriously. It all seemed very well organized, and the only thing that spoiled potential enjoyment when I returned the following Sunday, hoping for a lazy day, was the half-hurricane that was blowing. Sand was everywhere, in everything, smothering the low juniper scrub, obliterating the roadway, deck chairs were becoming airborne, the shore was a heaving mass of sea, sand and bushes. There was general chaos. I was assured that this was most unusual for early June, and certainly on the first day I saw Platamona, life looked tranquil enough, with hardly a ripple on the water, and not a soul in sight for all those miles.

From there we continued to Porto Torres, once an important Roman town of 15,000 inhabitants, founded on an even earlier settlement, now dominated by the sight and smell of oil refineries around which probably much of the commercial life of the rather faded town revolves.

The area boasts the famous Paleo-Christian basilica of San Gavino, considered one of the finest in Sardinia, built on the site of an ancient pagan burial ground, which became the scene of an early Christian martyrdom. Gavino, a Roman commander in the time of Diocletian, was converted by two condemned Christians, Protus and Januarius, and suffered execution with them. According to legend exhumation of the bones in a later century was attended by miraculous phenomena, the church now being a place of pilgrimage. Tyndale, somewhat anticlerical as far as the Roman Catholic Church was concerned, described the still impressive building as having been constructed by the *Giudice* of Torres in the eleventh century: 'An assumption to a certain extent confirmed by the simplicity of the architecture, though it bears many evidences of subsequent alterations and additions. The roof, which is of lead, rests on beams, so placed that it does not touch the walls, and consequently admits light and air through the interstices, and other loopholes and crevices tell of the days when the church became a fortress against the attacks of Corsairs, from which it suffered severely. The two aisles are formed by 22 columns, eleven in each row, all of different orders and characters, lengthened or shortened, *ad libitum,* and dug up from among the ruins of the neighbourhood.

'His (San Gavino's) bones, as well as those of Protus and Januarius, were dug up in the crypt, with great pomp and ceremony, in the year 1614, under the superintendence of the ecclesiastical authorities of Sassari, and a Sard author, writing in the year 1841, enumerates the following, as evidence of the sanctity of these remains: "The portents accompanying the discovery, the musical harmonies heard in many places, the unexpected splendours appearing in the temple, the frequent perfumes emitted from the tombs, the number of miracles performed upon the devout, drawn by a supernatural force to venerate the sanctity of these bones . . ."' Tyndale, however, remained sceptical. Unfortunately, owing to being given the wrong directions, Luigi and I never got there, which was disappointing. However, on a subsequent visit, alone, the Basilica proved well worth seeing. Originally, standing by itself on a small eminence it must then have been even more impressive.

I had expected to find it solitary, aloof, but, in the heart of the town, up 24 steps, the church, its soft yellowish stone pitted with the weathering of centuries, is surrounded by dwellings; on the one side neat and comparatively modern, on the other old and primitive, the latter festooned with washing of all shapes, sizes and colours. At a communal trough a handsome young girl with lacquered pink toe nails stood scrubbing her legs and feet, having already doused her short black hair. A halfwit squatted beside one cavernous doorway, a mindless grin on his sad, empty face; by another, a small baby on her lap, sat an immensely fat grandmother watching me with an inscrutable expression in piercing black eyes.

Inside, the mellow shade of the walls was made glowing by the soft light from slender arrow slits of windows either painted or covered with golden yellow paper, some of which was peeling.

The aisles are roofed with stone, and the nave, extending un-broken from one end of the Basilica to the other is lined by the tall pillars between the rounded arches as described by Tyndale, all in varying conditions of decay or repair. But light no longer comes from space between the roof and walls as far as I could discern. At the eastern end a simple altar rests on a raised dais, behind which stands the Bishop's chair of dark wood. Opposing this, in front of choir seats at the western end on a high plinth a statue of the Saint sits astride a sturdy white horse. Against the northern wall, on a wooden boxlike erection, perhaps contain-ing the bones, lie effigies of the three martyrs, San Gavino in the centre in his officer's uniform. On the figure of each lay a freshly placed flower, the toes of all three are worn by the decorous touching of the faithful. Alongside, locked rails at the head of some steps lead to the crypt.

Mass is still said in the Basilica, electric candles on the pillars and loud speakers adding their modern contribution, while a notice on the door in four languages reminds women to be 'modestly dressed and covered-headed'.

From Porto Torres Luigi and I continued our way alongside the salt marshes to Stintino, a little fishing village of no more than 1,000 people, as clean and bright as a new pin, passing on the way the *Tonnara Salina*, the tunny fishing and processing area. A small twin-engined plane weaving in and out over marsh and sea suggested that tunny might be in the offing, even at that—for the industry—late moment. But our hopes were in vain. The long factory buildings were obviously closed and de-serted, the men elsewhere. Nothing stirred. In any case around mid-May are, in general, the vital days, with rarely much varia-tion.

When tunny are signalled there is tremendous excitement, men and boats being carefully positioned, each fisherman knowing his exact role, the long, strong nets laid as dictated by generations of experience to trap the fish as they storm through in their thousands near the end of their arduous journey across the Atlantic to spawning grounds in the Black Sea. The direc-tion they will take is never certain until almost the last moment, either they pass to the north, by Stintino, or south of Sardinia, by the island of San Pietro. One man is in command, the *rais*. When all is ready (at the beginning of May) there is a blessing by a priest, and during the brief period of almost only hours while the *mattanza* is in operation the speed and skill of all those taking part is said to be remarkable. Once the great fish, some weighing several hundred pounds, are churning the ever-reddening sea in the final trap net, the *camera della morte*, there is no escape. The man who slips and falls in, or is knocked overboard by the sweep of a struggling tunny's tail is in trouble. Gutting, cleaning and cutting up of the fish is immediate; the whole operation to achieve the processing of the catch while it is still absolutely fresh is said to be outstandingly efficient. The men earn good money while the *mattanza* lasts, and there are general regrets that the period is so fleeting.

Stintino window boxes were bright with flowers, in the main street two houses were being freshly painted, one apricot the other a pale blue-green, in front of the little *albergo* a couple of Swiss tourists drank beer and sunned themselves. The small harbour, almost encircled, with only a narrow freeway to the sea, was full of boats being cleaned after the night's fishing, and the thoroughness with which they were being scrubbed down was all in one with the appearance of the village itself. The catch had already been taken away and the only residue on the quayside was a couple of heaps of revolting slimy *polpo*, looking even less appetising than when cooked, and a few of the pretty flying fish who get caught in the nets as they lie asleep on the surface, 'wings' outspread.

In the middle of the harbour there appeared to be some floating slabs of wood. Enquiry revealed these as big, slatted boxes about six feet deep and long, and about half that wide, into which are put any baby lobsters caught in the nets with other fish. They are transferred to the boxes and left in the water for about a month to grow, after which they are picked out, well developed, and sold. Plenty of their natural food floats through the slats of their crates and they are brought out fat and healthy, as well as profitable.

The tidy streets had eminently suitable names: there was, of course, the via Tonnara, and in front of a small bay, where children were splashing gaily and young men were cutting through the sparkling water with powerful strokes, was a statue of Saint Peter, complete with key, in a road labelled via Lungomare Cristofero Colombo.

In the small, newish church we were lucky enough to find the priest. A little, round, grey haired man, with the worn cassock and bad teeth of his kind, he gave us a friendly greeting and was pleased and proud to show that his altar candles as well as side and chancel lights were electric. Padre Vittorio Brunas had come to the church seven years before this building had been constructed in 1936 by prisoners from the penal settlement on the island of Asinara, a short distance across the shimmering blue water, and a plaque on the wall announcing the date of the consecration bore his name. Behind the pebble glasses was a shrewd, humorous twinkle, the warm smile accepted much, understood more. 'Yes, I know all the people.' One was sure he did just that.

He showed us details of the painted ceiling with the arms of the Archbishop of Sassari, and we talked about his flock, and the tunny fishing, of which there had not been any this season. The tunny just had not come this way, but it was as well, the padre said, for the men had been on strike. Which he explained with an enchanting gesture of raised eyebrows and shoulders, both hands cradled on elbows, rocking gently within the circle of his arms all that the fishermen had wanted to gather in. 'The young men of today want more money, but they don't want to work for it, alas.' He shook his head rather sadly.

Though reluctant to leave Padre Brunas, from Stintino we went on to Capo Falcone at the extreme tip of the peninsula. On the horizon sun and sea shimmered as one, along the route shale glittered. There was rosemary, thyme and cistus by the shore, and a sea so pellucid that it was a vivid blue where it dropped to depths, completely colourless, the sand showing through like a white ribbon in the shallows. Overhead, the small, sweet voices of larks pointed this lovely day.

Cala Gonone—the rocks, and (*right*) entrance to the Grotta del Bue Marino

Oliena at the foot of its mountain—from Monte Ortobene

At the Festa di San
Pietro—the men of
Orgosolo

Mario Mattana's
grandfather and
grandmother—Orgosolo

Central cone of the *nuraghe* at Torralba

Bringing one down to earth was the sight of the prison across the water on the island of Asinara, a short distance away. Beyond it, an ancient Spanish watch tower stood on a spit of land, alone.

We had originally thought to lunch at Stintino, in the small, friendly *albergo*, but I decided it would be as well to try the hotel at Capo Falcone to see what it was like. In any case it was in a most wonderful position. Outside the large Hotel Roca Ruja three big Pullman buses suggested group travel, and there they were, English, Swiss and Italians, each about a dozen strong. A menu without prices, had I not been too careless to notice it, should have been a warning. It was too hot to eat much, but we enjoyed our meal of cold meat, salad, cherries then in season, a bottle of the local wine, and for me, a cup of coffee. One glance at the bill, however, and Luigi made a beeline for the *maitre d'hôtel*. What persuasion he used I never knew, but the bill was reduced by 2,000 *lire*. It was still 7,500 *lire* and, plus a tip, seemed excessive for what we had had. Not until we left did Luigi say chidingly that charges for meals in hotels included service, and still more ruefully, that if we had gone to the *albergo* at Stintino we would have had fresh lobster at half the price. As I was paying I felt that this was rubbing it in somewhat, and that such counsel was perhaps a little late. But I had learned my lesson.

*   *   *

Not least of the fascinations of Sardinia are the *nuraghi*, those unique, mysterious, truncated cone towers built of great blocks of stone without any bonding, the earliest of which are thought to date back to about 1400 B.C. Found all over the island, the greatest concentrations, together with the Tombs of the Giants, rock-cut tombs, sacred wells, dolmen and other monuments are in the north-west and southern central areas. But anywhere a turn in the road may suddenly bring into sight one of these tremendous piles, nearly always situated in a commanding position, and always, I was told, within signalling distance of one another. The largest *nuraghi*, intended as fortresses, complete with stout

E   65

walls, towers and wells, to which local inhabitants repaired in times of danger, could it is estimated, accommodate up to 300 people. And in her book, *Sardinia*, published by Thames & Hudson in 1963, Margaret Guido describes them as 'surely among the most impressive monuments remaining to us in pre-historic Europe ... as one gropes through the ill-lit passages and up the flights of steps within the thickness of the walls, one cannot feel other than amazement at the immense strength of the buildings and at the military ingenuity of the people who devised and constructed them. Only the enormous experience and manpower of the Carthaginian army could lead to their downfall.'

Official records at present indicate the known number of *nuraghi* as about 3,000. Margaret Guido suggests 6,500, while I have heard the figure put even higher, and an Italian encyclo-paedia suggests not less than 7,000.

Of all those I saw unquestionably the most impressive was the group of *nuraghi* at Sant'Antine in the plain of Giave, near Torralba, 25 miles south of Sassari, along that road to Macomer I had travelled on my first journey from Alghero to Olbia.

As we passed the point at which I had originally turned back olives began to give way to ripe corn, some already baled, the rest toast brown, covering hills and valleys. Alongside the winding road poplar trees and acacias yielded place to cork oaks and small pines clipped by the wind, leaning over the *macchia*. But today there was no wind at all, the sun blazed out of a cloudless sky. At Bonnanaro were cherry orchards and acres and acres of ripe barley; and at a crossroads where we turned off to the principal *nuraghe* a group of young women, all dressed in black, with shawls on their heads, sat close together in the shade of euca-lyptus trees, deep in conversation as they waited for a train. This is the main line between Sassari and Cagliari, the single track here parallel for some miles with the road. Most of the trains are two-carriage diesel affairs of a dull tobacco brown, and this one shortly fussed its way into sight. The day was already so hot that a large dog with the women just lolled against a tree trunk, hardly bothering to give more than a cursory 'wuff' at us and at a heavily laden bullock cart making its slow progress towards the village, the two big cream-coloured oxen plodding on and on under the inexorable weight of their heavy yoke.

We turned off down a long straight track leading to the strange, tawny mass of stone that lay ahead, railed off for protection against modern man and beast. A good deal of careful work is being done to prevent sites such as this from destruction, and a couple of men were engaged under the guidance of a young surveyor, Giancarmelo Melio of Torralba, who gave us a pleasant greeting and immediately put himself at our disposal.

This is an area of extinct volcanoes, and from some of these, particularly a large one not far off, is thought to have been brought the basalt used for building this main, as well as five lesser *nuraghi* that some distance away could be seen ringing the great central fortress. The latter, built with a complicated system of entrances, had arrow slits at regular intervals round the outer wall, each narrowing towards the outside, the whole marvellously constructed of the huge blocks of stone without any mortar. Niches and chambers in the tremendously thick walls gave the impression that each had been designed for an exact purpose. Heavy slabs forming architraves of doorways still lay as solidly as when they had been placed there perhaps 3,000 years ago. There are two wells in this *nuraghe*, and inside the main wall a tapering central tower three stories and 50 feet high dominates the whole landscape. Inside it a system of dim, narrow corridors and steep steps were obviously calculated to make the efforts of invaders both difficult and perilous. At the top are chambers leading inwards from the corridors, and from the highest point to which it was possible to climb the view seemed to go on for ever, beyond the furthest *nuraghi* on all sides to the distant mountains, peak beyond peak fading into silver mist in the far distance. In the blazing heat of noon even the larks had ceased their trilling, and the only sound was a hoarse squawk as a big grey crow flapped on its way, leaving the silence the more telling for its passing.

In a field, too far off for any sound to carry, a woman was working stacking freshly cut barley, sometimes wearily straightening her back, wiping sweat from her face with the back of her hand. And as I watched a horseman slowly came into view on a splendid chestnut. Even at that distance one could see the red-gold gleam on the beautiful animal. The rider sat easily, erect, and the horse moved so smoothly that as man and beast passed from sight through the long grasses down a small incline they seemed almost to have been a mirage in the shimmering heat.

Against the outside walls of the *nuraghe* a broken pillar and traces of square buildings have been identified as of late Roman origin, and a labourer engaged on the repair work was marking stones as he moved them. Though he probably knew little of its history he was proud of this great edifice, admiring its strength and the inferred might of those who had built and lived in it. Easing a battered old hat from his brow he gazed up at the tower. '*È molto forte. Le piace?*' he demanded. I agreed with him about its strength and said I thought it a wonderful building, whereupon he gave a satisfied grunt and went on with his work.

Clinging to the red-brown walls were dozens of crickets whose speckled colouring offered almost perfect camouflage to human eyes, though not to those of an agile bright green lizard who, with a sudden dart, almost before one had realized it was there at all, had seized a *grillo* in its mouth, and with a wary, triumphant gleam in its eyes made off with its prize too quickly for me to focus my camera in time, only the final wisp of its tail being visible in the negative.

Our young guide was anxious that we should see the dolmen and a Giant's Tomb—'only over there'. Luigi sensibly elected to remain in the shade, but I stumbled after Giancarmelo Melio through the thick grass and a carpet of flowers, getting caught in brambles, scrambling over broken walls that looked as if they had been built of stones from the *nuraghe*, over granite outcrops hidden among roots, perspiration trickling into my eyes and blinding me as I staggered faithfully on. But it was worth the effort, for suddenly here was the dolmen, and close at hand, under a stunted ilex, the great elliptical granite stone, about nine feet high, with deeply incised border and cross bar, marking the tomb, thought to be the burial place of a whole family or perhaps of a clan. The original semicircle of stones in front has been dispersed, and the ground-level entrance was blocked, as was that of the dolmen, but it was all, with the *nuraghe*, part of a strangely moving, lonely scene. Once this great plain had been teeming with life. What had all these Sards been like? How had they lived—how, and where, died?

Beautiful orange lichen covered the dolmen, the uprights of which were about four feet high, the cross stone twice that length and at least 18 inches thick. Margaret Guido suggests that there are about 40 such dolmen throughout Sardinia, and that these, intended for single burial, preceded the *Tombe di Giganti*, built subsequently for multiple burials.

The richness of the still green grasses in the plain in mid-June was said to be due to an underground river, and as we returned along the dazzling, pot-holed *strada bianca* we stopped at a well to drink from a long stone trough through which flowed delicious ice cold water. According to local legend the supply has never failed and comes from the same stream that must have supplied the great *nuraghe*.

On the way back we passed Thiesi, its terraced hillsides a not very common sight in Sardinia, beyond it tall poplars and euca-lyptus led to Bidighinzu, an artificial reservoir into which water drains from surrounding hills, to be piped to Sassari. Pale rose and white rock through which the road was cut changed to the deep red of porphyry adding still more to the sombre atmosphere of melancholy that always seems to invest drowned land. Along the way we met several more riders of horse or donkey, and on a leading rein the one and only Castel Sardo donkey I saw. Of a special diminutive breed, established for centuries, they are hardly larger than a full grown retriever, their slender legs, soft ears and ravishing eyelashes enough to soften any heart.

Ittiri proved a cheerful village, with groups on the shady side of the street sitting round tables outside a little *albergo-ristorante* which we decided to try, and which proved entirely satisfactory. There was water in the taps upstairs, and the bedrooms, shown to me courteously by the *padrona* were simple but spotless. She cocked an enquiring eye at me for comment and when I said I thought they were very nice, and *molto pulito*, meaning much more in common usage than merely quite clean, she beamed. She had lovely regular features, large velvet-soft eyes, and the warm, buxom friendliness that casts a glow. She was, moreover, an excellent cook. We ate salami with artichoke hearts as a first course, Luigi then tucking into a generous portion of roast sucking pig that looked absolutely delicious, crisp and tender, good as was the salad we both had, which, together with fresh home made bread, butter, beer and coffee, cost just under £1 for the two of us.

We left well content, to seek a woman famous all over the province for her exquisite embroidery, and her skill in the making of costumes, the Ittiri dress being particularly elaborate. After some time we found her, but she had given up the work three years previously and had even sold her own costume. No more were being ordered, she lamented. Real gold and silver thread had been used in the embroideries, the young didn't want to learn any more, and a single costume took so long to make and was so expensive that girls were no longer planning such dresses for their weddings, to be handed down to their daughters in turn. She shook her tired grey head, and gave that expressive shrug of thin shoulders so full of meaning, of acceptance.

Part Three
*
NUORO

For the third time I set out on the Macomer road, this time on my way to Nuoro, and though from a map this may look a good example of the old tag about the longest way round to get the shortest way there, in fact, it is much the best route to take. The road surface is excellent—this is part of the new *autostrada* linking Sassari with Cagliari, and in addition, it passes through some glorious country.

Though it reaches across from east coast to west, as do the other two provinces, the western portion of Nuoro consists of little more than a corridor immediately south of Sassari that just includes Macomer itself, an important road as well as rail junction. From the centre the Nuoro province then sweeps down the whole eastern half of Sardinia, south of Olbia, and includes within its borders the three districts of the Barbagia: Ollolai, Belvi and Seulo; in them the fabled mountains of the Gennargentu that are not only the highest in the island, but represent the heart of Sardinia, refuge in ancient times of those Sards who fled from invaders rather than yield to subjection, and who were the founders of the mountain-top villages of today. It is the cradle of legends, of rare as well as more common flora and fauna, of black and white magic, the home of a great many law-abiding citizens and sometimes, as of yore, the hiding place of bandits, a term embracing a variety of men and their deeds, all too easily and sometimes carelessly applied.

The eastern coastline is the steepest in Sardinia. Below the granite cliffs white sands stretch for miles, often enclosed in small bays behind which pines, oleanders and *macchia* form a protective collar. All the way are grottos and caves in some of which have been found traces of Stone Age inhabitants.

* * *

Towards Torralba several horsemen were moving across the countryside. As before, the horses, mostly chestnuts, looked proud and well cared for; less fortunate travellers bestrode little donkeys who made steady progress apparently without difficulty laden with saddlebags as well as riders. Occasionally a bullock cart creaked its slow way, and always the man atop gave that sudden, brilliant smile and raised a hand in greeting in response to a wave that said '*buon giorno*' from me. The leaves of poplars and eucalyptus trees shivered in a light breeze that wafted bits of cottonwool cloud across the intensely blue sky, and as the kilometres clocked up the scenery grew wilder, bigger, higher. The air was like champagne.

Just before Macomer a series of hairpin bends led up and up, through a huge escarpment that looked as if giants had bitten a chunk out of it. On top, on all sides, the view was magnificent, an irregular checkerboard of corn, some still to be reaped waving gently in the light airs, some cut and stacked in dark golden bundles, the rest already carted, leaving a criss-cross of stubble edged in places with the dark green of myrtle and of other scrub, and always bounded on the horizons by mountains. High overhead the flickering wings of a falcon boded ill for tiny prey perhaps hiding below. In the near distance the small, lonely figure of a man was visible, the sweeping rhythm of his scythe so regular that there was almost a clockwork unreality about him.

I stopped to gaze and some minutes later a lorry pulled up alongside. '*Va bene, signora?*', called the driver, a grizzled man with beetling brows and tired eyes. '*Va bene, grazie*', I replied, and with a smile and a wave he went on. This had happened before, and was to happen again. Whenever I stopped on the road, unless I was out of the car and obviously taking pictures, the driver of any vehicle, and once a farmer on a donkey, stopped to ask if all was well, or if I needed help.

Presently the road dropped slightly to short, dry grass dotted with a straggle of cork oaks interspersed here and there with scrub, and as decoration scattered groups of the pretty mouse-coloured Sardinian cows.

In the long main street of Macomer I stopped for petrol. So many people were about, and such was the coming and going through those plastic fringes shrouding shops that I concluded it must be market day. From the adjacent railway came the sound and smell of the arrival and departure of a train.

In Roman times Macomer was an important military centre as well as road junction, and it is now an area of considerable archaeological interest which I would have liked to have had time to explore, but I had had to make a rule with myself that when travelling from one base to another there really must be a limit to stops, otherwise I never would arrive.

Near Macomer a rock shelter, S'Adde, was excavated not many years ago, albeit rather inexpertly, and in addition to pottery Margaret Guido records the digging up of stone arrow-heads and axes among a number of articles that included two important figurines of basalt, comparable with finds in the Landes and the Dordogne, suggestive of traditions brought not only from France and Spain, but also from Africa. There was also found the neolithic 'Macomer Venus', now installed in the Cagliari museum, one of the impressive treasures in that fascinating place which I saw on my several visits later.

Though it feels higher Macomer is only just over 2,000 feet up, but leaving the town and now travelling eastward the road wound round and up still more to yet another and larger plain, wilder this time, strewn with great lumps of granite outcrop in between *macchia* and short, old bent pines and oaks, the effect of this empty, windy, solitary place spoiled to some extent by a tangle of telephone poles and wires lurching in all directions. Further on the road dipped down by a river garlanded with pink and red oleanders; in a field a lone man in the traditional magpie costume of black and white was tying together heads of ripe barley not yet cut.

Approached from the west there is little to be seen of the town of Nuoro until one is almost on it, though coming from other directions it stands out stretched along a ridge, some 1,800 feet up at the foot of Monte Ortobene, but lower than the ring of mountains surrounding it across wide valleys. With a population now of nearly 24,000 it is the capital of the province and of the Barbagia Ollolai.

The Jolly hotel there is comparatively small, and of fairly recent construction, situated at the western end of the town among much new building going on in the form of solid-looking square blocks of flats and offices. This Jolly had the familiar features of its fellow *alberghi*, and from my room at the back was my first sight of Monte Oliena to the south, its Dolomitic mass, bleached and powerful, rising to just over 4,000 feet, always beautiful, always changing according to the time of day, the light and the weather, most beautiful of all rising rose-pink from the silvery mists of early morning, and in the evening when the glowing reds and golds of the setting sun slowly faded, leaving the silhouetted, jagged ridge wrapped in the still, blue shadows of coming night.

*   *   *

Having unpacked and sorted myself out I went down to lunch to find to my dismay a group of mixed French and Italian travellers I had fondly imagined were left behind at Sassari, where they had made meal times hideous with noise and clatter, and with demands that kept waiters incessantly on the trot. Now here they were, in a much smaller room, making an equal amount of noise, with, as usual in such cases, one man dominating the scene, the wag of the party, showing off his (limited) knowledge of languages and customs, smoking his pipe and trying to organize the waiters, too. At one moment at dinner that evening he tried to start his fellow travellers singing, but that was quietly and firmly dealt with, to my relief. The only thing that seemed amusing about this noisy irruption was the alarming way some members of the party—about a dozen in all—waved their cutlery at each other in conversation. I wondered what would happen if one or other really did get over-excited.

74

Before lunch I had already discovered that Doctor Bacchiddu, Director of the tourist organization, was away on holiday, that the *Presidente*, a *medico*, was *molto occupato*, and that one of the staff, Bruno Piredda, of whom I knew through the London office, was away ill, though expected back on the morrow. So having eaten, I decided to explore the town, to try to discover if D. H. Lawrence's street was still there, and the hotel from which he watched that Sunday *festa* when the young men of the town had been dressed in an astonishing variety of feminine costume, and rollicking fun had been enjoyed by all.

In *Sea and Sardinia*, written and first published in 1921, less than half the book is devoted to his six days in the island, and Lawrence reiterated firmly that he was tired of 'things', in the opening sentence of his book declaring his interest: 'Comes over one an absolute necessity to move'. Which resulted in masochism that required the taking of the cheapest kinds of tickets for himself and Frieda, the 'queen-bee', as he called his wife, to travel across a comparatively primitive mountainous island in mid-winter, where tourists were rare even in summer. Whether he exorcised his demon by means of the rigours of his journey is one thing; there are moments when the book becomes irritating, when his explosive petulance makes tiresome reading. The Sards, as well as Lawrence, were people with definite ideas, and it might have been amusing to have been able to have their re-actions to this eccentric stranger suddenly tramping aggressively in and out of their remote and frugal lives, the q-b trailing behind with the kitchenino.

But Lawrence was a genius, and if at that moment he was not at all interested in 'things', meaning history and its mani-festations, he could observe and bring to life the smallest detail of human behaviour, as exquisitely as he could describe the strength and sweep of a wild landscape, the beauty of a single almond blossom. As far as the people he met were concerned, it is his description of the night the travellers spent at the inn at Sorgono that is one of the passages most often referred to. But for those who know Sardinia the scene conjured up of that 'thin brown stalk' of a woman left behind on the station platform, her lugubrious husband glooming helplessly in the train as it gathered speed; and the absurd charade on a Sunday in Nuoro are even better, the latter a marvellous description of the Sard sense of humour.

'We pulled open the latticed window doors', he wrote, 'and looked down on the street: the only street. And it was a river of noisy life. A band was playing, rather terribly, round the corner at the end, and up and down the street jigged endless numbers of maskers in their carnival costume, with girls and young women strolling arm in arm to participate . . . The maskers were nearly all women: so we thought at first. Then we saw, looking closer, that most of the young women were young men dressed up. . . . It was quite a game sorting out the real women from the false. Some were easy. They had stuffed their bosoms, and stuffed their bustles, and put on hats and various robes, and they minced along with little jigging steps like dolls that dangle from elastic, and they put their heads on one side and dripped their hands, and danced up to flurry the actual young ladies, and sometimes they received a good clout on the head . . . They were very lively and naïve . . . Every conceivable sort of "woman" was there, broad-shouldered and with rather large feet. The most usual was the semi-peasant, with very full bosom and very full skirt and a very downright bearing. But one was a widow in weeds drooping on the arm of a robust daughter. And one was an ancient crone in a crochet bedcover. And one was in an old skirt and blouse and apron, with a broom, wildly sweeping the street from end to end. He was an animated rascal. He swept with very sarcastic assiduity in front of two town-misses in fur coats, who minced very importantly along. He swept their way very humbly, facing them and going backwards, sweeping and bowing, whilst they advanced with their noses in the air. He made his great bow, and they minced past, daughters of dog-fish, *pesce-cane*, no doubt. Then he skipped with a bold, gambolling flurry behind them, as if to sweep their tracks away. He swept so madly and so blindly with his besom that he swept on to their heels and ankles. They shrieked and glowered round, but the blind sweeper saw them not. He swept and swept and pricked their

76

thin ankles. And they, scarlet with indignation and rage, gave
hot skips like cats on hot bricks, and fled discomforted forwards.
He bowed once more after them, and started mildly and inno-
cently to sweep the street. . . . There were some really beautiful
dresses of rich old brocade, and some gleaming old shawls, a
shimmer of lavender and silver, or of dark, rich, shot colours
with deep borders of white silver and primrose gold, very lovely.
I believe two of them were actual women—but the q-b says no.
. . . There were two wistful, drooping lily sisters, all in white,
with big feet . . . These maskers were very gentle and whimsical,
no touch of brutality at all. . . . One youth wore a thin white
blouse and a pair of his sister's wide, calico knickers with needle-
work frills near the ankle, and white stockings. He walked art-
lessly, and looked almost pretty. Only the q-b winced with pain:
not because of the knickers, but because of the awful length,
coming well below the knee. Another young man was wound
into a sheet, and heaven knows if he could ever get out of it . . .
It was a river of noisy life.'

Lawrence's narrow, cobbled street is still a busy thoroughfare
in the centre of the town, among a maze of old alleyways, now
mostly one-way streets. The café on the corner is there, too, in
the Piazza Crispi, the via Dante shooting upwards at one side
towards newer buildings. On the other side a road drops through
the Corso Garibaldi and the main square, rather faded and
lacking something of the liveliness of the smaller one, though it
is filled with stalls, paper kiosks, the taxi rank, petrol station, and
inevitable seats, the resting places of older men in their sad rows.
As in varying degrees in every Sard town or village, barbers'
shops, bars and tobacconists predominate, but scattered among
these in Nuoro were also signs of the times, in shops selling
refrigerators and television sets. A draper's window held the
most revolutionary sight of all—a very blonde model in a full
length white satin wedding dress, with tulle veil and white satin
slippers.

Expensive cameras were to be had, and jewellers' windows
showed the traditional gold filagree work. Two book shops were
treasure houses of all those additional things to be found in such

places, as well as of books, and the courtesy and interest of those who served tempted one to make excuses to go again. I wanted Carlo Levi's book on Sardinia: *Tutto il miele è finito—The honey is Finished*—and a fellow customer commented that this was a marvellously poetic work in his opinion. He did hope I would like it. Next time I went in the *padrone* remembered me, and wanted to know if I had yet had time to read the book, did I like it, had I read that other work—*Christ stopped at Eboli?* When I said not only had I read it, but that I had been to Eboli, everyone in the shop joined in what became an animated discussion, and led inevitably to the usual questions. Was I alone, why, where had I been, where was I going? Did I like Sardinia? Ah, but did I know any *Sardi* well? The reply, yes, to the last two questions brought pleased murmurs and several helpful suggestions. A week later, and some 20 odd miles away, near Dorgali, I was suddenly greeted with a broad smile and '*Buon giorno, signora*'. It was one of my acquaintances of the bookshop who wanted to know if I had yet read my purchase.

* * *

Nuoro is proud of its literary personages, Sebastiano Satta, the poet, and, particularly, Grazia Deledda who was awarded the Nobel prize for literature in 1926 for her novels dealing with *Nuorese* life. Though much of her time was spent in Rome with her diplomat husband, Giovanni Madesane, she was born in the town of Nuoro of 'quite ordinary' parents, attended the local school, and suddenly, at the age of 18, began to write: 'In exercise books, in longhand'. There was little need for invention, here at hand were the deeply-rooted power and passions of primitive, isolated peasant peoples living in an ancient, wild countryside, where faithfulness and endurance were among essentials for living, where inherited prejudice could spell triumph, but more often disaster; where knowledge of black and white magic, of good and evil, was none the less powerful for being hidden.

Love for and understanding of her countrymen and women

was in Grazia Deledda's blood, and her talent was probably just in time, before the canvasses began to be blurred by the approach of the rapidly developing modern world. And though her style has in it much of the nineteenth century, it is fitting and is wholly at one with the slow-moving inevitable fate of her subjects. Reminding one of Thomas Hardy, and sometimes of George Eliot.

Two of the best of her books are considered to be *La Madre*, and *Canne al Vento* (*Straws in the Wind*). The former is a tale of a widowed mother whose son, a young priest, has fallen in love with the local rich woman and of her fatally destructive power over him. The opening paragraphs describing the pathetic mother sitting in her room in the dark, work-worn hands still moist with the washing-up water, straining to hear the faint movements that will tell of her son's stealthy exit from the house, lead inevitably to the final scene in the church. The mother, having succeeded in separating the pair watches the woman advance to the altar where, in revenge, she has threatened to denounce her lover. At the last second her courage fails and she remains silent, he collapses, but the strain is too much for the unhappy, exhausted *madre*, who dies, but whose death effectively separates the pair for ever in their secret guilt.

Canne al Vento is the history of an old serving woman, poor, ignorant and faithful, and the disruptive elements of greed and jealousy in the family for whom she works, and of her communion with the spirits of the river banks.

The authoress herself, who was born in 1871 and died in 1936, lies in a tiny chapel, *La Solitudine*, now dedicated to her at the foot of the road leading to Monte Ortobene. Inside, whitish-blue walls are broken by small, high windows; beneath, shallow alcoves repeating the line of the windows break the severity of the walls, and in one of these, on the south side, is the plain, black marble sarcophagus engraved with her name: Grazia Deledda. That, and no more. The altar is simple, a grey marble basin holds Holy Water at the main entrance, the floor is of chequered black and grey stone, and in the alcoves hang three-dimensional bronze plaques representing the 12 Stations of the

Cross, matching in style the bronze door at the western end of the chapel.

It was a tranquil place, the only sounds the chirruping of small birds wafted in with the scent of surrounding pines. Outside, a man lay asleep, stretched out on a bench in the golden light of afternoon. But the following Sunday evening around the seat was a litter of discarded ice-cream cartons.

*   *   *

The next morning I betook myself to the via Ballero, to the offices of the tourist organization in the hopes of finding Bruno Piredda. Curiously enough almost all the tourist offices I saw in Sardinia were neatly tucked away, with little more than a discreet doorplate or the like to assist bemused travellers to find them. Unlike the Jolly organization, for example, who put signs at the entrances and exits of towns to indicate the whereabouts of their hotels. One could not help feeling that similar enterprise on the part of official bodies might be very helpful to strangers seeking information.

Bruno Piredda was at his desk. Small and frail-looking, in his youth one of the victims of malaria, he proved to be the kindest and most gentle of men, with an encyclopaedic knowledge of his province in particular, and of Sardinia in general. His own personal contact with Britain in terms of actual journeying was restricted to a brief visit in 1943, when, as a prisoner of war taken in North Africa, he was brought to Glasgow to embark on the Queen Mary for the voyage across the Atlantic. But like others I met in similar cases, he bore no grudge—it was the fortunes of war, there were worse things. After the first few occasions I ceased to be embarrassed. What could one say but—'Oh, I'm sorry. I hope it wasn't too bad', or some such triviality. With true Sard lack of inhibition the information was generally conveyed quite cheerfully, even with pride if sojourn in Britain or on the American continent had resulted in some knowledge of English, however limited.

I had hoped that Bruno Piredda would have been able to

accompany me on one or two forays, but unfortunately in the absence of Doctor Bacchiddu it was felt by the President that he could not be spared, even for a day. There was much work on hand in connection with the annual Feast of the Redeemer, on August 29th, work that involved coping with an influx of pilgrims from all over the island, and this was now less than three months away. But of his store of knowledge and understanding Bruno Piredda was ever more than generous. It was also through him that I had the good fortune to meet Gianetto Licheri of Orgosolo, who invited me to visit him and his family there. When I later asked Bruno Piredda whether this was to be taken seriously the reply was: 'Certainly. If a Sard invites you to his home he means it.'

Meanwhile I was recommended to try the *ristorante* Fratelli Sacchi, as being *tipico*, at the top of Monte Ortobene, where true *Sardi* dishes were served. This proved to be another 1,500 feet up on a route that spiralled, lined with oleanders, broom, lilac and blackberry blossom among other flowers, behind these, fig trees, pines and ilex, and beyond those the green of juniper and myrtle among the dried grasses. A fresh breeze swept white clouds across the blue sky, and as I climbed panoramas opened out, spanning 360 degrees, picture postcard views of mountains and valleys on every side, shimmering through the heat. To the south the pale mass of Oliena gleamed through its blue haze, standing out conspicuously from darker tree-mantled peaks to right and left. Further south still the great bulk of the Gennargentu massif loomed, silver-blue layers in the distance, fading into misty nothing.

Nearly at the top of Ortobene the ESIT (*Ente Sardo Industrie Turistiche*) hotel, in a marvellous position, looked rather new and self-conscious. Beyond, round a small public garden, are several *ristoranti* and one or two private villas. At the very top is a big bronze statue of The Redeemer, underneath it a stone altar, the focal point of the later pilgrimage. On the morning of August 29th long-distance buses from all over the island converge on the town of Nuoro, and in the afternoon a great procession led by the Bishop, priests and choir makes its way to the summit, followed by men and women in their varied and beautiful regional costumes. A service of thanksgiving is held, and later comes the merrymaking, with traditional songs and dancing. At midnight the buses return whence they came, and for another year the great day is over. At the turn of the century this started as a genuine pilgrimage, now it is in the way of becoming a tourist attraction.

At Fratelli Sacchi's all was peace on this day and I was duly installed on a narrow, sheltered terrace. Straight ahead lay Orune, draped over its small peak like a shawl. Away to the north-east stretched the Albo range, and almost due east a faint line suggested the sea at the edge of the Golfo di Orosei. Fluttering round the blackberry flowers and on the purple wild sage blossoms butterflies looked even more fragile than ever against this tremendous backcloth of scenery. And to the scent of sage was added that of rosemary and thyme, mingling with the delicious aroma of sucking pig and baby lamb roasting before a wood fire on the traditional vertical spits in the open courtyard in front of the *ristorante*.

I ate Sardinian smoked ham, sucking pig with salad, enormous, luscious cherries, washed down with the red wine of the house, light and refreshing. And once more the idea that the *signora* took her coffee *amaro* was a habit for wonderment—with a slight shudder. The wine was served in litre bottles with a sort of ginger-pop stopper, from which one helped oneself. I couldn't open the thing, and at last a man sitting at a table near couldn't bear my fumbling any more. He rose. 'Scusi, signora.' With a flick of the wrist he opened the bottle, indicating how easy it was, once one knew how. Then with a smile and a little bow he returned to his table and his own female companion.

It was here, too, that I was introduced to the famous *Carta da Musica*, wafer-thin bread made of special *Sardo* corn, the *grano duro*. The preparation and the baking is a complicated affair taking a whole day, but the result is not only very good, it has remarkable keeping qualities, and is the traditional bread taken by the *pastore* when he wends his lonely way in spring and summer up to the mountain grazing with his flock of sheep or goats.

No one seemed to know the origin of the name, and one can only guess that it may have something to do with the fact that when the bread is broken (when baked it is the size of a large dinner plate) it gives off a sharp, snapping sound.

The little terrace was soon full and included a quartette tucking in with obvious pleasure. I imagined three to be of a family —elder sister, married, a handsome, buxom creature, younger sister, still at school, and a young brother, a little older, newly come to the priesthood, with a fresh, innocent face. The fourth member of the party was an older priest. Together they enjoyed large platefulls of *pasta*, following which they were served with *porchetto* and salad such as I had had. They were just settling down to this when there was a loud crack, a slight shriek, and elder sister slid slowly sideways from view, one hand aloft holding her fork on which was impaled a juicy morsel of meat. Her chair leg had given way. In the ensuing noisy mêlée several other men as well as her own companions leaped to the rescue, she was provided with another chair, and the party settled once more. Fortunately she was not hurt. What made it all quite fascinating was the way that fork remained firmly upright throughout, like a beacon. Reseated, without further delay she went on with her succulent piece of *porchetto* as if there had never been any interlude at all.

Elsewhere, three Dutch girls were having a happily hysterical time trying to order a meal with the aid of a phrase book. It reminded me of an occasion in 1946 when, with four colleagues, I was invited to Norway on an official visit. In the Dakota aeroplane of those days the journey took four hours, and we whiled away some of the time studying a phrase book sensibly brought by the most resourceful among us, Evelyn Irons, one of the best journalists of all time. '*Tak vor marten*' was not difficult, though later we found its utterance governed by certain complicated etiquette. But we never did find any use for the first two phrases—'Fred, where are you?', and 'Do you like pea soup?' I wondered if the Dutch girls' booklet at Fratelli Sacchi's was in similar vein.

I had finished my meal in a quiet corner by the entrance to

the *terrazzo* and was awaiting the bill when three young men arrived. Standing by my table they were obviously disappointed to find the place so full, so I suggested that if they cared to be patient for a few moments I was shortly leaving, and perhaps they could sit here. They thanked me politely and we chatted as we waited. One, from his accent and in some way from his bearing, I thought to be from the *continente*, and having answered the usual questions myself—yes, I was a tourist, alone, no this was not my first visit. Yes, I liked Sardinia, *moltissimo*, no, I was not French, I was English— I asked if they were all *Sardi*. One said he came from Nuoro, the second was from Sassari, the third, from Rome. And were they on holiday also, I asked? They looked at each other in silence for a matter of seconds, then one replied, no, they were police. Anyway, my change had arrived and I rose to go, bidding them '*Buon appetito, signori, e buona fortuna*'. The Roman chuckled: 'She understands.' One of them I was to meet again, under very different circumstances.

Halfway down the mountain was an inviting open space, sloping down to the valley on the other side of which was spread Oliena, at the foot of its mountain, a rare happening in this region especially where villages were rather set high under the rim of a peak, safe and inaccessible from centuries-long enmities. I tucked the car into a shady niche and found a pile of cut bamboos on which I lay, at peace with the world. To the myriad other scents here was added that of fig trees warmed by the sun, there was the sound of trickling water, and in the oak under which I rested birds were fussing a little. The cause, I thought, might be the hawk soaring on eddies in the bright sky, then hovering with that incredible flicker of wings before the lightning, death-dealing swoop. But either it had missed, or had made a mistake altogether this time because it soared up again, like an angry brown dart, and presently disappeared.

Returning to Nuoro I decided to visit the *Museo Regionale del Costume*, south of the town, sited on a small hilltop, the Colle San Onofrio. The word *Regionale* can be misinterpreted, because though some of the exhibits are local, the costumes themselves come from all over Sardinia, and this is intended as the national centre for them. None too soon if our experience at Ittiri is at all general.

Built some six years previously to the design of a well known *Sardo* architect, Antonio Simon Massa from Sassari, the museum is laid out to resemble a small traditional *Sardo* village, complete with chapel and well, and with street names in dialect. There is the *Arruga de is Prateris* (the Goldsmiths' street), the *Patiu de Cresia* (the Church Square), *Sa Domu Campidanesa* (the country cottage) and so on. Additional developments are planned, but present buildings include a concert hall with facilities also for film showings. The whole concept simple, elegant and effective, with the main exhibition rooms on slightly different levels, avoiding the usual long, bleak look of many such buildings. The actual collection was only started three years ago and is still limited, but the wealth and fascination of what is already there augurs well for the future.

Costumes include a *Nuorese* wedding dress for both bride and groom, the girl's consisting of the usual long, accordion pleated skirt of crisp wool, this time black, edged with a 12 inch band of fuschia red moiré silk. Slit sleeves of the embroidered jacket were open to show the big balloon sleeves of the white cotton blouse beautifully embroidered and smocked, with fine hand-made lace edging, held at the neck by the double cone-shaped gold filagree buttons one sees all over the island. On the bride's head is a small, square embroidered cap. The man is dressed in the black and white outfit of white cotton shirt and long, full pants tucked into black felt leggings and worn with that curious, cropped, full, black wool garment neither trousers nor kilt that stops short halfway between thigh and knee. He wears a sleeve-less black sheepskin jacket and the famous stocking cap, the beretta, that so intrigued D. H. Lawrence, in this case hanging down one side.

Lawrence describes these caps with great enthusiasm: 'The long stocking caps they wear as a sort of crest, as a lizard wears his crest at mating time. They are always moving them, settling them on their heads. One fat fellow, young, with sly brown eyes and a young beard round his face, folds his stocking-foot in three, so that it rises over his brow martial and handsome. The old boy brings his stocking-foot over his left ear. A handsome fellow with a jaw of massive teeth pushes his cap back and lets it hang a long way down his back. Then he shifts it forward over his nose, and makes it have two sticking out points, like fox-ears, above his temples. It is marvellous how much expression these caps can take on. They say only those born to them can wear them.' Lawrence's comments would still seem to hold good, judging by what I saw. This headgear is a splendid expression of the nonchalant individualism of the Sard male. It is also an inheritance from earliest days, bronzes found in *nuraghi* and now to be seen in the Cagliari museum showing men wearing something very similar in shape.

Other costumes in the museum included an elaborate wedding dress from the Campidano region in the south—red velvet and rose and yellow brocade, the groom wearing a matching waistcoat; and costumes from Osilo, Orgosolo and Oristano, each different, all beautifully made, some with shawl or veil hiding mouth and throat, a fashion perhaps inherited from Arab invaders.

There are finely wrought silver belts, coral ornaments and gold filagree, beautiful hand made rugs and horse furniture for festas dyed brilliant shades with vegetable colourings. A *cassapancha*, the traditional family coffer of dark chestnut wood, expertly carved, spinning jennies, including an example of split bamboo incised with poker work, and silver and bronze reliquaries, together with a pile of Roman coins and Spanish eighteenth-century pistols with chased silver handles, are only some of the treasures. Old terracotta ware, some partly glazed, is alone worth seeing, like so much else on view designed and made not only with skill and taste, but also with wit. A water jar is shaped like a monk with piously folded hands, and head bent under the cowl, but in some subtle way there is a hint of mockery in the figure; a cottage oven has a model of a man with a wickedly humorous face sitting on the lid; there are other water jars shaped like birds, with a soft greeny-yellow glaze, beautiful both in colour and texture.

Each of these mountain villages has an *ambiente* all its own, not least Oliena. From Nuoro the road drops sharply, winding to the valley, and a right hand turn takes one over a bridge spanning a small fast-running stream tumbling from the mountain, bordered with oleanders, alongside olive groves and vineyards. The red wine of the district is known throughout Sardinia, and the poet d'Annunzio sang its praises. I found it light, pleasant and refreshing.

As I stopped to gaze at the scene a ring dove was calling softly. There is no mistaking that gentle voice; it was the first time I had heard it, though they are quite plentiful in the province.

Oliena itself, mostly of grey stone, looked forlorn in a way that is not apparent in mountain villages with their sweeping views. A few children were playing round the petrol pump and a water trough. Communist slogans chalked on walls included *Pace a Vietnam*, and on a ledge sat the usual row of old men, several in the black and white costume, wearing their stocking caps, each at its own angle.

I asked for the home of Emanuele Ghisu, a young surveyor to whom I had an introduction, and promptly there were offers to show me where the house was, in the Piazza San Lussorio. The door was wide open, and as I could not see either bell or knocker I climbed the marble stair to the first floor, there were no rooms at ground level. Emanuele Ghisu's mother came to greet me. A matriarch, with scanty grey hair drawn into a bun at the back, framing an oval face that must have been lovely once, now she had the weary eyes and malarial skin of her generation, but she carried her bulk with a gentle, unruffled dignity, and bade me welcome, drawing me by the hand into a small, neat sitting room. Emanuele, summoned from his office above, arrived in the company of a rumbustious friendly kitten that fluttered round his feet and everything else like a wayward feather.

What could they do to help me? It was very hot, would I care to have something to drink? It was the signora herself who brought delicious cold beer. Of her family of five only Emanuele, a lean, handsome 23, and Paulina, a little younger, equally good looking, were at home; Antoniana was married and living in Nuoro, the elder son was a *professore* at a Rome agricultural college, and Cecita, the youngest, was still at college. The father, small and bearded, whom I met later had, I thought, something to do with farming.

Tomorrow was the *Festa di San Giovanni*, said Emanuele presently, when people made a pilgrimage to local chapels, then continued on to the picnic by the river, and it was the custom, when they met at crossroads, to forgather and drink each other's health, before continuing on their different ways. If I would care to visit San Giovanni we could then go on to Monte Tiscali. Nothing could be better, so next morning I returned to Oliena, and presently we set out, with the addition of a young friend of Emanuele's, Angelino Floris, a journalist. I was never quite sure why he was included, whether this was a matter of etiquette, or just for the fun of the trip. In any case it didn't matter. They were equally charming and amusing.

So far the weather was not promising. Only a fitful sun lightened the heavy air, clouds wrapping the peaks on either side as we rocketed, Emanuele driving, over the rough *strada bianca*. Presently we came to a little chapel set back from the roadside, among vineyards, and stopped to exchange greetings with friends and relatives. Special small cordial glasses were produced and large bottles of the famous *vernaccia*, a somewhat, potent wine, generally drunk as a liqueur and very popular with the *Sardi*. One could imagine that meeting many friends during such a journey could possibly have a cumulative effect, but my impression was that these were decorous, friendly, family outings, without much likelihood of untoward happenings. Rigid conventions rule such lives, the women hung back, and it was for the most part the men who did the talking, as head of the family. Children were shy but nicely mannered.

I was introduced to the wife of a *Nuorese* schoolmaster who, with her daughter and granddaughter were leaving the chapel as we arrived. Family resemblance between the three generations was the most complete I have ever seen. As well as facial likeness, even the small, chubby girl of four had something of the aura of complete serenity that invested the grandmother. What was particularly interesting was the reaction of my two young companions. 'Isn't she beautiful' they said afterwards. She wasn't any more, in the classical sense of the word, but it was obvious what they meant and felt. I agreed.

Continuing our way we came to a *trattoria* at the end of the road. In the garden a river poured out from a high, rocky cavern. Limpid and cold it flowed quite fast to spread out, winding between shallow, sandy banks and under a high bluff at one side, wild mint adding its own quota to the scent of oleanders and other flowers growing from every niche. With some ingenuity a narrow channel had been made through which some of the stream had been diverted to flow over cases of beer laid in a long row in the water. It was a splendid cooling system. The water was also delicious to drink.

Little family groups came and went, wandering through the garden, children eager to watch the water flowing ceaselessly from the dark, mysterious heart of the mountain into a deep pool formed by the continuing cleft in the rock before it tumbled over to spread as the shallow stream beyond. In the shade of a eucalyptus plantation by the bank one or two family groups of women were settling themselves and chatting, big baskets suggesting adequate provisions. Under the rocks on the opposite side of the river their men were busy building a fire and preparing stakes to be driven into a little clearing at the water's edge. They were joined by two more, one the local butcher, each of the pair carrying sucking pigs ready for the spit. The cooking would take about two hours, meanwhile there was a lovely smell of woodsmoke, to which would soon be added that of the roasting meat. There was wine for any who were thirsty, the *trattoria* if more, or beer, was needed, and the rest of the day to talk, to laze or to sleep as inclination demanded. Some of the men knew Emanuele and invited us to come across. He led me carefully over the steep, slippery rocks, not at all easy to navigate, but I made it, hands reaching out to help over the last drop. The men, about nine in all, had that air of decisive masculinity about them, of resilience, so noticably a hallmark of the Sard, and that Lawrence found so satisfying. Unselfconscious and friendly, I found these, as others of their island, the easiest of strangers to meet, with a natural dignity that was good to encounter.

Tyndale comments on this quality more than once, and tells a story of an obviously poor shepherd who left his home and meal to guide the traveller for some three miles across country: 'After showing me the spot, and sharing a light meal, I offered him a trifle for his trouble, but he indignantly refused it, and on leaving to return home, gave me an adieu with a fervent but courteous demeanour that would have shamed many a mitred and coroneted head.'

Our return across the water was not all that dignified, however. We decided to take a short cut, and Emanuele, leading the way, pulled and laid some of the reeds flat into the water to smooth my passage. He did his job so well that I slid off them straight into the stream, and but for his restraining hand would have gone right in. Roars of laughter came from our friends on the other side, and Emanuele and I were ourselves laughing so much I could hardly scramble out even with his aid. I had only gone in up to the knees, and wore unlined canvas shoes with rubber soles, so the damage was not great, and, indeed, the speed with which both shoes and trousers dried was some measure of the heat of the day and dryness of the atmosphere generally.

From San Giovanni a jagged, stony track wound up to Monte Tiscali, on one side sheer over a steep, green valley, on the other, in the lea of the heights through which it had been cut. It was nothing if not vertiginous, but suddenly the road turned abruptly and we were in a wide, flat valley, almost completely surrounded by mountains. The clouds had disappeared and the hot sun, beating down on this strange remote place without a breath of wind, turned it into an oven. Ringed by *macchia*, beautifully cultivated olive plantations and vineyards in serried rows promised a rich harvest. This is *terra comunale*, to which agricultural workers are brought in official buses and, as shelter for them, a short row of single storey stone cottages was tucked into a small enclosure at the foot of a ridge.

It was also a paradise of birds and flowers, and for the first time I heard a sound I had been waiting for—the cicada—true signaller of the south. There were bright finches galore, ring doves cooed softly, and suddenly a hen partridge darted from under a bush to cross the track, frantically urging on her five babies who followed in a protesting line, the smallest and last falling over a pebble in its anxiety, reducing the hen to what must be bird hysteria. Some at least of the reason for her agitation became apparent with the sight of a forbidding shape hovering in the sky above. But whether our presence deterred the falcon, or something else, it soared away, to my private relief.

Monte Tiscali loomed in the background, a sugarloaf peak, and down a rough path to the right lay the *Grotta su Vento*, a huge cave, said to be one of the longest and deepest in the island. The entrance to it lies across an extraordinary mass of tumbled, rugged boulders, dotted with low bushes, and to know how these rocks came to lie in such a fashion might be to know the answer to a number of archaeological and historical questions.

Emanuele and Angelino Floris skipped across this barrier as nimbly as their own goats, of course, but I followed more slowly, lost in wonder at the beauty of the pinkish-gold rock leading into the shadowed cave. At the entrance were traces of a recent fire, but there was no other sight or sound of human presence that I could detect. Inside, here and there light filtered through cracks showing ledges in the lofty dome, and a passage narrowing away to the left through which a stream ran, cold and deep. The air was beautifully fresh and continues so for miles, I was told.

Traces of pre-Nuraghic villages have been found in the valley, '*molto B.C.*', said Emanuele. Margaret Guido describes the site rather more fully: 'Perhaps the strangest of all the mountain retreats is at Monte Tiscali . . . on a rocky peak is an immense karsitic cave, now open to the sky in the middle; presumably the roof fell in in ancient times, as the huts built inside the cave are placed on each side of the fallen rocks. The walls of these huts, of which there are both round and rectangular ones, are unusually thin; even so, many of them still stand to a considerable height, making the huts look like little towers. Excavations have revealed that this village was occupied in the Roman period, and indeed when the classical writers referred to the Sardinians as living in caves in Punic times, they may have had in mind just such places as Monte Tiscali and the gallery *nuraghi*. According to Didorus Siculus and Strabo, it was only possible for the Carthaginians to take Sardinians prisoner when they temporarily left their hide-outs to go to public feasts and assemblies.'

Whether this author is actually referring to Monte Tiscali itself, where there are also caves, or to the *Grotta su Vento* is not clear, but the latter would appear to be larger.

Emanuele reported having several times seen groups of up to 20 *muffloni*, the now rare horned mountain sheep, on Tiscali, but as we did not have the time to climb the heights I was not fortunate enough to see even one. These are now protected by law, and there are several large herds among the higher peaks of the Gennargentu, also. But we did see some quite splendid goats on our way down. Suddenly they shot out from above, on the near side, rushed over the rocks and across the road to disappear absolutely head first straight down into the valley. Even for these beasts it seemed an unusually precipitous passage, but not a bit of it. I peered gingerly over the edge and there they were, thrusting quite composedly into some bushes. The *caprone* was a beautiful fellow, large, with sweeping curved horns and a shining silver-grey coat of long silky hair.

Back in Oliena the family had obviously had their meal, but insisted that I stay and eat with Emanuele. He remembered that there was to be a wedding the next day and suggested I should come and see it. The bride would be in traditional costume, as would be a number of her relatives and friends. Apart from the interest of the event itself, the Oliena costume is held to be one of the island's best, so of course I accepted the invitation with the greatest pleasure. The Signora Ghisu disappeared, to return with her own costume to show me.

In her case the usual full-length accordion-pleated skirt was of a deep red-brown, woven of a mixture of wool and goat hair, making it not only wiry and virtually uncrushable, but very long lasting. At the hem a 12–inch border of white satin was beautifully painted with a design of roses and other flowers. A special paint is used for this, a form of decoration occasionally replacing hand embroidery. With the skirt was a cotton blouse of ice-blue, in its turn, smocked, and finely embroidered at neck and cuffs of big balloon sleeves. Over the blouse is worn a brief bolero with sleeves tapering to the wrist and split to take the billowing sleeves of the blouse. Open at the front the brocade jacket repeated the design of roses and other flowers on the skirt band. Completing the outfit was a short, black lace apron, and, for the head, a small fringed shawl of fine wool matching the colour of the skirt had one corner exquisitely embroidered with gold thread in an embossed pattern. The head shawl is worn folded diagonally, with the edge rolled, giving the effect of an upstanding coronet. Fastening the blouse are always the traditional double cones of gold filagree, in addition to which it is a matter of prestige that the wearer also has other gold filagree and coral jewellery, mostly in the form of necklaces. While the final seal to a wedding is the heavy, square, gold signet ring engraved with his initials presented by the groom to his bride, as well as an ordinary wedding ring, and quite apart from any earlier—funds permitting—jewelled engagement ring. The signora showed her own signet ring with pride, bearing now the honoured scars of some 25 years wear.

Paulina, too, brought her dress to show me, which she was in the course of making; in this case the white satin band was being embroidered to a design only lightly stencilled on. Of the part already done colour and workmanship alike were quite exquisite. Such outfits take two or three years to complete, friends sometimes helping each other, and I asked Paulina how long hers would take, but she only gave a shy downward-looking smile and said she didn't know. So I left well alone, wondering if some young man had or had not yet popped the question.

Emanuele, engaged to a *Nuorese* girl, now working as a hospital nurse in northern Italy, whom he had recently been to see, remarked wistfully that it cost a lot of money to get married and set up house, and that wasn't easy to come by. But he hoped to get married in about two years.

Alas! The wedding day dawned overcast, with a blustery wind and spitting rain. Having been warned to be punctual I arrived at the appointed hour, without having realized that this was not intended to be taken too literally. The family were hardly up, and Emanuele did not appear until some minutes later, with a sheepish, apologetic grin.

I had hoped the Ghisus themselves would be among the guests, and that would have meant me, also. This was obviously not to be, which was disappointing, but bearing in mind the thin ice on which I might be treading in this land of centuries-long *vendetta* and rigid family protocol, I refrained from pressing the question. Meanwhile Paulina kindly produced coffee for us all, as we watched a certain amount of comings and goings from their balcony.

The wedding pair, Assunta Corrias and Mario Puligheddu were both of Oliena, and presently there appeared walking with grave dignity through the village street a small procession of about twenty men, with some half-dozen women, one or two in costume, bringing up the rear. This was the bridegroom, supported by his family, going to fetch his bride from her father's house. Mario Puligheddu, bareheaded, tall and handsome, in the centre of the front row, with a brother either side, all three in ordinary dark suits, with white shirts and plain ties. Preceding them walked three small children hand in hand, two little girls in white, frilly dresses, and a little boy in a blue suit, the tots on the outside proud bearers of white wands on which were tied white ribbon bows.

Arriving at the bride's home the best man would step forward and ask the father for his daughter. He, the father, then makes a little speech pointing out that he has done everything possible for her—as a symbolical reminder to the younger generation of family responsibilities—and inferring that the bridegroom had better do likewise or there would be trouble. She is kissed away by all her family, and in some villages is carried to church either by her father or a brother, or, if the bridegroom is well to do, he may fetch her on his horse, setting her up behind him.

This time the procession came on foot, led by the groom with his bride on his arm, her family and friends now accompanying his to the church. They made a remarkable pair by any standard, Assunta Corrias, tall and slender, gravely beautiful, though obviously a little pale and tense walked with a dignity and grace that was moving. Her costume was similar to that of Signora Ghisu's except that this bride's skirt and head shawl were black, and the embroidered white satin band on her skirt had a narrow edge of crimson.

Towards the end of the service the bride's married sister left the church and took up her position at the foot of the steps, in what had been her own wedding dress, which she had made. Similarly she had helped with the present bride's. Now she waited with a plate in her hand on which were rose petals and grains of wheat—'*sos granos*'—the special Sardinian corn, the two together symbol of happy, fruitful marriage. As the pair emerged from the church and led the way down the steps other friends appeared, bearing similar plates the contents of which were flung at the bride, and the plates were then dashed to the ground, part of a very ancient custom, said Emanuele.

A shaft of watery sunlight glinting on the gold of the bride's shawl made a halo round the proud, shy head as with a faint smile she stopped to rearrange it a little. Then, composed and dignified she and her husband led the procession once more back to her old home.

All the girls and women wore similar gold-embroidered head shawls, but apparently only the married ones the full costume, and the contrast between the short, swinging skirts of the younger members of the party, and the rich tokens of another age in the older women was not quite an easy one, for all that the girls wore their shawls so unselfconsciously. What was particularly noticeable was the free, upright carriage of nearly all of them.

Back at the bride's home there would be toasts to the couple, refreshments taken by all except the newly married pair, and following more short speeches, the custom is for friends now to help carry the wedding presents, all of which are sent to the bride only, to the new home. After which everybody finally repairs to the bridegroom's father's house for the banquet, where the man's family have to give as good a show as they can, to prove how fortunate the bride is in her marriage, and that her husband is well able to provide for her.

*　　*　　*

There is a well known and ancient expression in Sardinia: '*Il vero Sardo*,' 'the true Sard.' It remains one of the enigmas of the island, so far one of the continuing mysteries, seemingly impossible to define exactly, but which is generally taken to refer to a certain type of man or woman, only occasionally met with, and then generally in the province of Nuoro, who are obviously of a quite different race from their fellow islanders. Notwithstanding the obvious fact that over the centuries the blood of several different nationalities has been mingled with that of the original inhabitants, particularly in coastal regions where it is still possible any day to meet with a profile pure Greek, a keen Arab face, traces of the skin and eyes of other Africans, to name only a few.

In Nuoro again after the wedding I was suddenly reminded of this, finding myself face to face with an example of what was surely *Il Vero Sardo*. Many *Sardi* are small people, but the couple coming towards me along the Corso Garibaldi were unmistakable, and utterly different. Dressed in the usual clothes of country folk they were tiny, not stunted, just very small boned, with round heads, high flat cheekbones, and with almond eyes, dark and different. It was fascinating, and I made a detour, going back on my tracks in order to confront them again unobtrusively. Their separateness marked them out as though they were in a frame. I only met one other similar couple during my journeyings, these some distance away, in the Barbagi Belvi, near Aritzo, equally unexpectedly. Equally, these, too, stood out, a people apart.

So far the question whether they are the true descendants of the original inhabitants, as yet unidentified with any certainty, has never been answered finally. But adding interest to the existence of such people is that there are words still to be found in dialects, particularly place and other names, that do not owe allegiance to any known tongue, three of which I came upon later in Desulo.

* * *

The *maestrale* appeared to have blown itself out by the following morning and I went up again to Ortobene, wanting in particular to take some pictures of the *porchetto* roasting on the spits. The young Signora Sacchi was pleased to co-operate, but asked me to wait a few moments until she had finished what she was doing, which she insisted was most important. This was quite a business, bits of skin and fat of the carcases to be cooked being rolled up in several layers of brown paper, then tied tightly with rows and rows of string. Wondering where all this was leading to I waited in some private impatience, to be confounded when, the parcel completed to the liking of the *signora*, she stuck one of the spit rods into it, thrust it into the heart of the wood fire, and held it there. In due course the whole thing became a flaming mass, and the burning fat dripping from the packet was then held over each side of sucking pig in turn, to baste it, ensuring that the wafer-thin crackling would be crisp and succulent. I felt suitably humbled, which didn't lessen my eventual pleasure when it came to lunch time.

A little group of men and boys taking a Sunday glass of beer watched my activities with interest. Presently, very courteously, one asked if I would take a cup of coffee with them. We chatted, and eventually, of course, came the usual questions. Did I like Sardinia? When I said yes, very much, that I was only sorry not to have a companion who could tell me about the area, they promptly offered the name of a local *professore*. 'He is elderly,' they said, 'and poor, but a writer and a historian, and he knows the region very well indeed. He hasn't got a car, but you have, and he might be able to help you greatly.' He was '*molto, molto gentile*,' they added, in reassurance, and saw to it that I wrote

G

down the name and address of the *professore* correctly. I promised to get in touch with him before leaving, which unfortunately was to be soon, and though the next few days were likely to be fully occupied. Indeed, I certainly would have done so, had there been time, which, in the end, there wasn't.

By late afternoon the wind was back again, and considering plans for the next day I decided that unless it was calm I would not go to Dorgali to see the caves, as suggested by Bruno Piredda. Instead I would take Gianetto Licheri at his word and visit Orgosolo, going via Oliena so that I could take some flowers to Signora Ghisu.

Monday morning, however, was bland and beautiful, with not a breath of wind, so off I went to Dorgali, and Cala Gonone, on the coast, about fifteen miles away. The route follows the road to Oliena until that right turn when it continues straight on instead. The sun blazed down, few trees shading this route with the exception of one huge olive, said to be about three hundred years old, under which already sheltering from the morning heat stood a flock of sheep in a tight huddle. The temperature generated by their bodies in such a packed mass must have been appalling, but this was obviously their chosen spot, and four days later when I passed again, there they were, just as tightly jammed, looking as though they had not moved at all.

To the right Monte Oliena still dominated the skyline, pinkish in the bright morning. Cicadas were rasping away. Olives, vine-yards and scrub ran right down to the verge of the road until, on a curve, it swooped up in a series of hairpin bends, climbing Monte Dorgali—not very high—with oleanders like a rosy rib-bon dropping down all one side marking the passage of the little river Cedrino. On top were more olives, girdled by old, dry stone walls being repaired by a couple of men in company with a cheerful mongrel. I stopped a big bullock cart to ask the driver if I might take a photograph and the two teased him, demanding of me why I wanted to take such a picture: 'He's only a poverty-stricken farm worker,' they jeered, and all three laughed good-humouredly. I said I liked country life and country people anyhow, and I thought the great oxen were beautiful, at which they all laughed uproariously at such a preposterous idea, on which cheerful note we parted. It was the only vehicle, apart from mine, on the road between the Oliena turning and Dorgali. The second time I went back, a few days later, the pair were still working on the walls and recognized the car as I approached, calling a greeting and raising a hand in salute.

Dorgali was once a Saracen settlement, but much older are the many nuraghic remains in the area. At a sharp turn marking the entrance to the village was the largest mimosa I had ever seen, at least twenty feet high, a glorious mass of perfumed, golden-yellow blossom. I pulled up to look at it, and asked a couple of passing *carabinieri* the whereabouts of the *Pro-loco* office, the local branch of the tourist organization. 'If I may come in your car I will show you, *signora*,' replied one. In he got and a few moments later pointed out the office, suggested a good parking place under a tree, gave me a huge smile as he climbed out, a smart salute, and went on his way.

The little office was as neat as the brisk young man in charge. Behind his dark glasses Nicolino Porcu proved immediately helpful, offering then and there to take me to Cala Gonone on his motor scooter. Had I come by bus? I said I had come by car and perhaps we could journey in that, and in no time at all we were away, the road, hairpin bends as ever, winding through terraced vineyards to a tunnel through which we emerged to find the sea glittering below. Three newish hotels were grouped round the small port among a few private villas, and having chosen a spot that would remain shady we left the car and went immediately to a group of fishermen on the quay. They were discussing with some astonishment a young tunny fish that, quite out of season, had been brought in by one of their number with the night's catch, and now, roped by the tail was swinging uneasily in the water beside the boat. They shook their heads at the havoc it had wrought in the net.

One of the fishermen cleared ropes and tackle from the bottom of his boat and we climbed in. It was an ancient craft with a tiny engine in the centre that, with disproportionately loud explosions and much oily smoke, was presently coaxed into continuous life, and we chugged across the bay. Small and lean, Mario the boatman could have been any age from thirty to sixty. Beneath a curly thatch greying at the temples he had the face of a battered eagle, with a crooked beak of a nose, furrowed cheeks and nutcracker jaw. A straw hat that had once been vivid with rainbow-hued horizontal stripes was tilted forward to shade dark, deep set eyes narrowed to slits in the brilliant light reflected back from the dazzling blues of sea and sky. He took the first puffs of a cigarette offered by Nicolino as a starving man might have been savouring meat and drink, drawing smoke deep into his lungs.

We made for the *Grotta del Bue Marino*, dialect for the Grotto of the Sea Ox, in other words, the seal's cave, where, deep under the cliffs live the only seals still to be found in the Mediterranean. Grey, with white fronts, as a species they are said to be survivors of the Ice Age; as such, quite unique, and now protected by law against the depredations of hunters.

There was still some swell following days of wind, but even so, at a depth of fifty or more feet every ripple in the pale sand was visible, details of every plant growing at the bottom and several varieties of small fish. In little bays, solitary and inviting under beetling cliffs fringed with scrub and low oaks, the white sand was untrodden. Elsewhere, down to the water's edge and below, extraordinary striations of rock swirled this way and that, varying from the completely vertical to almost horizontal, in their different colourings hinting of the wealth of minerals with which the island is endowed. Overhead, sea-gulls nest, openings to smaller caves mark the whole coastline, and above the entrance to the main grotto as we arrived swallows were wheeling.

We glided gently in to be met by Francesco the guide who lit his miner's lamp and led the way into the dark interior, lighting as we went Butane gas flares placed strategically all along the route, and as carefully extinguishing them when we retraced our steps.

The entrance to the grotto is astonishing enough, but immediately inside sharp purples give way to patches of brilliant sulphur yellows and viridian green. As we made our way along the railed path to the inner caves leading from one into another I could hardly believe my eyes and scribbled in my notebook 'A cross between Aladdin and Wagner.' It is.

A river leads off to the left from the confluence of fresh and salt water. To the right the way opens up through chambers filled with stalactites and stalagmites, some joined to form great columns, the variety and size of which were so unbelievable that one had almost to touch them to be sure the colours and textures were real and wouldn't rub off. Glistening obsidian crystals, a shining white calcined deposit on rose-gold rock, alabaster—pink, white or warm yellow—completely translucent when Francesco swung his lamp behind, and other coloured quartz, all were grown, are growing, into shapes large and small, some as fantastic as others are beautiful. There were tiny human figures, animals of many kinds, including one looking like some huge prehistoric lizard apparently climbing up a wall. There was a shimmering formation, creamy-pink, known as 'the wedding cake,' another, 'the crowned Madonna,' small and exquisitely grown in the living rock, there were lilliputian forests, as well as columns a dozen or more feet high. The forms were endless. Adjacent to a fragile-looking alabaster shape hung a great reddish stalactite that was very hard and rang like iron when tapped.

Everywhere the air was pure and cool, and as we made our way from gallery to gallery, still, deep lakes of fresh water looked dark and sinister. A few are known to contain fish. Where the sea had once penetrated but has now receded the walls of chambers are deeply pitted, suggesting a high water mark at one time considerably above present known levels.

The fresh water stream extends back to the limit so far explored, nearly five kilometres, and in the furthest cave of all is the seals' *rifugio*, from which they emerge at night or in the dawn to catch fish and to swim in the sea. Spelaeologists working in remote caves the day before reported having seen some of them, though I was not fortunate enough to get that far, but Francesco said he had often heard them, though never actually seen them. Yes, he insisted, they were there all right. Did he himself find the grotto fascinating, I asked, or did he now know it too well? Big, dark eyes were fixed reflectively on mine. It was a wonderful place, he said. He liked it when he took people who really were interested, but it was very tiring to have to make two or three trips a day with tourists who were not very interested after the first few minutes. It must have been. We were there for only a couple of hours or so and I was nearly dropping when we emerged, to find Mario sleeping peacefully in the bottom of the boat. For a moment, as he wakened, his eyes opening wide in the shadow of the cavern were as young and innocent as a child's, then the world of knowledge and memory returned.

I had invited Nicolino to lunch with me but he had begged to be excused on the grounds that he would like to take the opportunity of being here to see a friend, which was understandable. So I ate in solitary state one of the best lobsters ever to be put before me, ordered by Nicolino as we passed on our way to the boat. Served with crisp salad and a pleasant enough dry white wine, *Nuraghe Majore*, from the Alghero region, followed by fresh peaches, it made a delicious meal eaten out of doors in the shade of a bamboo awning. After which I lay stretched out in a long chair watching the sea, almost hyacinth blue in the early afternoon light, until Nicolino returned to collect me.

Dorgali is a centre for carpet making, terracotta ware and gold filagree work. But though I was never able to see any of the last being made anywhere in Sardinia, and not for want of asking, on our return we did find several women at their looms weaving the traditional rugs of undyed white wool. One, herself elderly, was working away at a small hand loom that had been her great-grandmother's with a skill that one wished could have brought her higher rewards than she probably earned. Yes, she answered, the design was inherited, too, painstakingly worked out on graph paper with the aid of now faint pencil crosses. A stout cotton warp is used, undyed wool for the weft, the result being a three-dimensional pattern that is not only good to look at but is said to be very hard wearing.

It was late in the afternoon and the potteries had ceased work for the day. The industry is very old, the ware being decorated with primary colours or black and white, in traditional designs of animals and geometric figures inherited from an ancient and unrecognized past. Adults had all gone home, but there were several children around, boys and girls, who said they helped with the decorating and in other ways after school hours, and in the holidays. They did the honours charmingly, with grave wide-eyed courtesy, showing everything with pride, including two kilns, one old and wood burning, the other, indicated with suitable emphasis, a new gas-burning oven that was, we were assured, '*molto forte*'. Nothing appeared to be locked up, neither were there any bolts or bars as far as we could see. Reminding one, not for the first time, of Lawrence's comment on the obvious honesty of the population of Sorgono.

Returning to Nuoro the clear, golden light of early evening etched the mountains fold on misty blue fold to a diminishing silver haze of distant ridges under the great dome of the sky, promising, I hoped, another lovely day on the morrow. Oliena gleamed rosy at the summit until the last shaft of light had gone.

The portents were only partly true, the sun shone brightly enough next morning, but the *maestrale* was back, and I thought with pleasure of my luck yesterday to have had such calm weather for the trip.

Rashly I decided to take the direct, shortest route to Orgosolo. It proved to be an awful dirt track, the sandy soil eroded on both sides by winter rains, frequently making it difficult to avoid going over the edge one side or the other, or into potholes. But the road lay through a fertile valley broken by rolling hills and I ceased to regret my temerity, enjoying the sight of the green vineyards facing south, the orchards, the flowers and the distant views between the trees. Twice I met *carabinieri* carrying their rifles at a business-like angle, their jeeps parked in the shade, and I wondered idly if the game they sought had four legs or two. The last lap over the crest was covered with cistus, before the final sharp turn that revealed Orgosolo like a narrow thread laid just below the top of its mountains.

Old grey stone houses were perched on ledges up and down winding, narrow, cobbled lanes, window and door frames painted vivid pinks, greens and blues. In a few cases whole houses were so treated. There were a number of people about as I moved slowly down what was obviously the main street, and coming towards me a couple of short, middle-aged men, one plump, one lean, both clad in dark grey suits, with trilby hats tipped forward over their eyes. They were deep in conversation but I pulled up and asked if they could direct me to the house of Signor Gianetto Licheri. They gave me a searching, doubtful look, glanced at my number plate, then, questioningly at each other. There was the slightest pause before Plump Grey Man spoke up. Yes, he knew where the house was. Bidding me park the car in a niche he indicated, surrounded on three sides by a stone wall, as I climbed out he told me to lock it. 'Children are sometimes curious,' was his reason.

Together, in silence, a certain inexplicable, suspicious tension in the air, we walked a few yards down the street to stop in front of a double door. Plump One rang the bell, and we waited, still silent. They obviously did not wish to speak. To a maid who came something was said in *Sardo* that I did not understand, and again we waited, again in silence, until within seconds Gianetto Licheri appeared. In his twenties, tall, dark and handsome, he came forward with outstretched hand and beaming smile. 'Welcome, *signora*.' Instantly the tension eased. All was well. I was accepted. Gianetto greeted the two men, then shook a rueful head at me. 'You've come at an unlucky moment I am afraid,' he said, 'yesterday a Dutch journalist was shot here.'

'A what? Where?'

He pointed. 'At 10.30 in the morning, down there on the Oliena road.' For a fleeting moment the wind blew chill. This was precisely where I would have been about that time had the *maestrale* still been blowing, in which case I would have come here instead of going to Dorgali.

'He is Cristopher Johannes Scherer. He was staying at the Jolly at Nuoro over the weekend. You must have seen him, a big, fair chap,' added Gianetto, 'with a Volkswagen.'

104

I did remember Scherer, having seen him by his car alongside mine, and again, in the restaurant.

So this was why, as a stranger, I had not at first been welcome in the village.

At the bottom of the valley, coming round the mountain from Oliena, just before the road darts up to Orgosolo, in full view of the latter, there is a very sharp hairpin bend with a slightly difficult camber. Here, at the beginning of the turn a masked man had tried to intercept the traveller, and two more had appeared from behind bushes. Scherer had put his foot down on the accelerator and tried to get away, but had been met with 'a hail of bullets' as he swung his car round the curve. He had managed to continue up the road to Orgosolo before collapsing, moaning: '*banditi, banditi.*' A villager seeing his condition and realizing that he was bleeding had run for the *carabinieri*.

The 46-year-old bachelor from Amsterdam, in Sardinia to collect facts for magazine articles, was now in Nuoro hospital, where he had been found to have been wounded in the shoulder. He would recover very soon, fortunately. And the rest was conjecture at the moment. Except for the report that the object of the attack was thought possibly to have been to obtain a 'getaway' car with an unfamiliar number plate, to be used in a robbery of the Bank of Sardinia in Orgosolo, or the Post Office, where a large consignment of money had just been received.

There was no question of the disapproval and regret of my three companions. This offended one of the most basic principles of Sard life—of hospitality to the stranger, and for the second time within recent memory.

'Now, of course, when foreigners talk about Sardinia they will think of Orgosolo, and imagine we are all thugs,' said Gianetto, glumly. The other two nodded agreement, but Thin Man added a rider. 'He should have stopped,' he said severely. His point was understandable, with his knowledge of his own countrymen, even if it didn't seem entirely reasonable to me. Given an unarmed man in a car confronted by three armed robbers on foot trying to stop him, I felt the Dutchman's reactions had been normal as well as quick and courageous. But I held my peace.

The story was in the morning paper, they said, which I had not yet seen, hence my ignorance of the affair. I had, in fact, realized that something was going on in the hotel the previous evening. There were newcomers in the restaurant, three men with sharp, thoughtful eyes, all obviously preoccupied. Two were at one table, a third, with a woman, at another. Each had been called away more than once during the meal, and in reply to something the husband had said on his return, the wife had hissed in obvious astonishment: '*una giornalista*'. I had not thought any of them looked like either tourists or commercial travellers, and had wondered who this journalist might be, but had not been very interested, and had left shortly and forgotten the incident. Now it was explained, and as it turned out later, all three were police.

My two Grey Men were cynical. 'They never will be caught. They never are. Just look at those mountains,' with a wave of the arm that took in the whole countryside. I asked myself if it was always the countryside, or how much of it was possibility of a *vendetta*, how much centuries-long loyalties.

The two discovered from Gianetto that I was British and Plump Man announced with a commendable accent and with aplomb: 'I spik Anglish not so good, but understand. I no practise so much.' Here was yet another prisoner of war. We chatted amicably about what London was like compared with Texas, whither he had been transported with comrades. Texas, he found 'too big at all,' which, comparing it in size with Sardinia, was understandable. Presently with smiles and handshakes we parted, and Gianetto turned to the business of being host to me.

I would stay for lunch, please, but first of all he would take me to the top of Monte Orgosolo and show me the village. Afterwards, if I liked the idea, we would go to San Giovannio, the topmost peak hereabouts.

He excused himself for a moment to let his mother know of my arrival, then off we set, to the top of Orgosolo. Though the wind had already travelled across half of Sardinia from the north-west, it still had the freshness of a sea breeze, and was not at all cold. It was easy to understand how this site had grown into a village; on all sides for miles the approaches could be seen, beyond them lay the ring of mountains. Far below the fatal road to Oliena twisted, on the clearly visible hairpin bend small ant-like figures were moving. 'Come on, we'll go down and see what they are doing. I know some of them,' said Gianetto. So down we went. The whole area was teeming with *carabinieri* and plain clothes men; when we arrived at the actual scene of the shooting a car was being photographed at the spot, and there also, very businesslike and very busy, was one of my three detectives from the Fratelli Sacchi *trattoria* on Monte Ortobene. He gave me a half smile and a quick nod of recognition on being introduced, then carried on directing some operation.

It was a lonely, well chosen place for such an endeavour, encircled by mountains, escape possible in several directions, where the sound of shooting might well pass unremarked as an everyday happening in a part of the country abounding in game, both feathered and four-legged.

In due course we arrived back for lunch. '*Dove la mama?*' de-manded Gianetto as soon as we got in. She was there, obviously waiting for us, though an elder brother had just finished because he had an appointment to keep some distance away. Beside her tall sons Signora Licheri looked tiny. Slender and frail in her widow's black, with delicate features in a small, pale face, she was gentle and kind, taking this unheralded arrival of a wind-swept woman in trousers apparently quite unperturbed. There were two more sons, one older and one younger than Gianetto, the elder to be married in two days' time in Cagliari, as well as a daughter, already married, the eldest of the family.

Gianetto proved himself a charming host, indeed had already done so, now with an easy grace that throughout the meal kept the conversation going between the three of us.

After lunch we set out for San Giovannio and the Fontana Bona. The way led up through the Prato Sant'Anania, a huge tableland of dry grasses dotted with small evergreen oaks and occasional clumps of myrtle, cistus and blackberries. The wind was full of the scent of flowers and of thyme. Small streams tumbling from the mountains make the pastures ideal for the cattle, goats and pigs that in summer all roam loose, only sheep are herded, and once or twice we saw a shepherd's hut in the distance. The *pastori* live up in these highlands with their flocks for several months at a time, taking with them when they go wine and their *carta da musica*, finding meat and water as they need it, milking the sheep and making cheese. In winter the animals come down to lower lands for shelter and additional food. In any case lambing has always to be watched for danger from foxes among other predators.

From the *prato* we drove through a bumpy, winding forest road to the mountain peak, passing a *cantonieri* house, the tawny building usually occupied by roadmenders, here the shelter for foresters keeping watch for fires. Schist gleamed, alternating with limestone rocks, and as we jolted carefully over the rough, narrow track, climbing to more than 4,000 feet, tremendous views opened out. Views with a difference. We were nearing the edge of the Gennargentu; Duluiscu loomed, bleak and bare, Oliena was almost hidden, but Monte Gonare—sugarloaf in shape—in the foreground, and even higher peaks fading away as far as the eye could follow, were thick with dark pines, with oaks and chestnut, interlaced with *macchia* below. The sound of trickling streams could be heard above the wind, the song of birds, and once or twice we saw the black pigs thrusting through the undergrowth; one piglet in particular grunting and grumbling away at its mother until she suddenly turned and in no uncertain voice obviously told it to cease. Which it did, instantly, now picking its way through the scrub in silence, with meek, downbent head.

As Gianetto was pointing out the various peaks I remarked that I supposed somewhere down there the three malcontents were hiding. 'Not at all,' was the crisp reply. Gianetto knowing his *Orgolesi* better than that. 'They are either at their usual work, or at home, wherever that may be.' It was possible, of course, that these bandits were from some other village.

Amid clumps of trees and a carpet of flowers, at the very top a small plateau was crowned with a bleached mass of rock on the topmost point of which a big, black and white goat with curving horns gazed down at us in the usual king-of-the-castle, supercilious goat manner. The wind was blowing half a gale here, but the sun was hot. This was primitive, lonely untouched land of tremendous strength. I was loathe to leave it.

We took a roundabout way back via Mamoaida, like others of its kind looking rather desolate in the late afternoon sun. Here at the time of their annual carnival paticipants wear extra-ordinary masks—'*Sos Mamuthones*', some absolutely grotesque, others funny, for which the village has been noted for genera-tions—relic of some long-forgotten pagan rite. Near the village is a single, small *nuraghe*.

The next day was the *Festa di San Pietro*, a public holiday, I had understood, everywhere. Gianetto laughed. 'Oh, in Orgo-solo we don't take any notice of that. We have our own festa.' Which he wanted me to see, and which would include a *cavalcata* late in the afternoon. Unfortunately, however, he had to leave in the morning for Cagliari for the brother's wedding, but he went to considerable trouble to arrange that two of his friends would look after me, Mario Mattana, whom I met that after-noon, and who was briefed to find and tell Mario Tomainu that he also must assist in taking care of me.

Just as I was leaving Gianetto laid a hand on the car door. 'Don't go back the way you came. Go via Mamoiada,' he said quietly, though no word had so much as been hinted of what was in both our minds. 'It is further, but there is some traffic on that road. You will be back before dark.'

So I took a thoughtful way along the ever-winding, longer route, knowing that I had to make up my mind without unduly dramatising the situation whether or not I was going to allow this latest shooting to affect my comings and goings. It had been close enough to be uncomfortable. But for the fact that the *maestrale* had ceased, the victim, or a victim, could so easily have been me. And my car was one of the very few in the neighbour-hood with a strange number plate.

It was no good kidding myself that the traditional courtesy to strangers, particularly to women, always operated. Just about two years previously a middle-aged couple named Townley returning from New Zealand to England via Kenya and Sardinia, among other holiday places, had been shot and killed on the outskirts of Orgosolo. Apart from a pair of binoculars neither had been robbed or otherwise molested.

I had, in fact, already discussed the affair with two different *Sardi* friends, one an official. Both told me exactly the same story, what they related does not agree with some versions I have seen published, but if what I was told is correct, not only is it logical in terms of local life, and very possible, it also means that perhaps to some extent the Townleys brought their own fate on themselves.

At that time there were known to be detectives in the neighbourhood, making exhaustive enquiries. One of them was a woman. The Townleys, wandering in the mountains came across a young man with a rifle. Without so much as 'by your leave' Townley started taking photographs of the man, who retreated, Townley following him into the *macchia*, still taking pictures. Obviously with something on his conscience the man continued retreating, the Townleys to follow him, whereupon the young Sard lost his head, apparently thinking the pair were police, and shot them. A few days later his body was found at the roadside with evidence that he had been killed in his turn because of his offence against the Sard code of hospitality to strangers. That this further murder started, or continued, a terrible, bloody *vendetta* is but a by-product of the tragedy. When I discussed the affair with the official, his comment was 'It was the justice of the people, instead of the justice of the Law. We were very, very sorry indeed about the Townleys.'

This is not to excuse the crime, but it may to some extent help to explain it. It also pinpoints an unfortunate habit seen in many countries where tourists roam photographing all and sundry, without ever paying the subjects of their pictures the courtesy of asking permission. By the same token slums are called 'picturesque', though that would not be the epithet in the travellers' own countries; the poor and the rich alike may be intruded upon with impunity because they are 'different', or 'fascinating', or 'cute' or whatever the adjective may be. Which is surely excessively bad manners, to say the least. Where tourism is now well established local people may have became inured to the habit, some even invite and be flattered by it. But particularly where poorer, unsophisticated countryfolk are concerned in re- mote areas, that strangers, presumed to be infinitely more affluent, should want to take pictures of less fortunate people is often felt to be a mockery, and as such, resented. Quite apart from the fact that in isolated communities, including some in Sardinia, there are superstitions involved that are widely and tenaciously held.

Bad manners are not grounds for murder, but among simple, primitive people, where blood is hot, weapons habitual, and prejudices strong, they can and do lead to terrible disasters.

*   *   *

Several *Sardi* words are used to describe what in general terms are now referred to as 'bandits', including *latitante, grassatori, malviventi, fuorilegge*, and, of course, *banditi*. Each has its own particular meaning, but even in Sard newspapers the last three are used fairly indiscriminately, though a *fuorilegge* (an outlaw) could be an innocent man, condemned in his absence, who has fled into hiding for reasons of his own rather than face what he may feel to be overwhelming, if wrong, circumstantial evidence, or if either of those two terrible words, *omerta* (silence), or *vendetta* are involved, or, as often happens, both of them.

Tyndale used the word *malviventi* almost exclusively, and described how one such band of men, acting on their traditional code of honour, rescued a lost and distressed traveller, taking him to the border of 'enemy' territory, handing him over for safe keeping to their rivals, and endangering themselves in the doing.

In Sardinia, banditry, if one can use the word as an omnibus term, can be divided sharply into two categories: the first, where foreigners are concerned, the second, among the *Sardi* themselves, or Italians who may become involved. As regards the former, so far as I can ascertain, the Townleys, a French couple who were fired on through a misunderstanding, but were not injured, and now, Cristopher Scherer, have been the only cases in recent years involving violence, and as such were deeply regretted by Sards in general. Around Alghero there have been several cases of hold-up, where holiday makers in night clubs or in buses have been robbed, but at the time of writing, so far at least, such victims have never been physically injured.

In the past, robbery or violence among the Sards themselves arose basically from one or both of two causes—hunger or *vendetta*. It is a fact that the 'have-nots' of the island really have not —still. A Sard newspaper in this connection quoting the fact that the annual income per head of the population of Orune, in Nuoro, was reckoned to be no more than £60. With the stocking cap and the *vendetta*, cattle stealing was an inheritance from the Nuraghic past, but once the taking of an animal as between *pastori* was an accepted part of the philosophy of life, that the man who did it was in need, and so to be tolerated, the *quid pro quo* probably following later. In the same mood there have been recorded cases where fellow shepherds have each contributed a beast from their own herds to aid one of their kind in distress. If robbery overstepped the mark that was quite another question, something not to be tolerated at all. Then trouble might and often did arise, which, once started, could continue for generations, on the basis of an eye for an eye, a tooth for a tooth. That situation, as well as relations between *pastori* and farmers, was unhappily acerbated in the late nineteenth century by the passing of what approximated to the English Laws of Enclosure, as a result of which shepherds often found themselves deprived of pastures they had long felt to be theirs by right of age-old custom, and the resulting breach has apparently never been really healed.

Now another element has entered into this unhappy situation, into these proud, almost tribal lives. Modern inventions, that within recent years in countries everywhere have changed not only physical living conditions, but have had a profound effect on moral values also, these are now influencing Sard existence, not less than life in other countries. And the physical changes in Sardinia in many cases are not, in effect, from the tallow candle, through oil lamps, then gas, to electricity, but directly from the flint to the jet engine.

Writing on the subject of the abduction of a business man for ransom, a Sard newspaper put a banner headline across the front page: 'Once they robbed because of hunger or *vendetta*, now it is for money to buy television and washing machines. . . .' Adding its quota to the situation is the fact that Sards rarely if ever do their military service in the island. Sent to the *continente*, or further afield, inevitably they make comparisons with conditions and opportunities at home and elsewhere.

In the island there is a well-known saying to the effect that Sicily has *Mafia*, but in Sardinia there is only *macchia*. The inference being that crime in the latter was neither organized, nor political, as in Sicily. That this state of affairs may be changing is perhaps indicated by such events as the kidnapping from an Olbia factory just before I arrived of Signor Palazzini, the young manager, in the middle of the night. He had been enticed there on a very plausible pretext. The abduction was not only well and carefully organized, but the Mayor of Monti, a village some fifteen miles distant, was named by the bandits as intermediary to handle a ransom of no less than some £14,000. Which was duly paid and the victim released, physically quite unhurt. But silent. There was a lot of cynical eyebrow raising on the subject when I was in the district, and I have not heard since of anyone being apprehended for the outrage, which it was suggested had to do with an affair of past politics. Though whether that is true or not I have no idea.

Likewise, several months later, the brutal murder of a farmer who had earlier refused to pay a ransom, but obeying the unwritten *Sardo* law of *omerta*, of silent loyalty, had, equally, refused to give information that might have led to the arrest of the *banditi*, and the more recent case of Cristopher Scherer, as well as a previous robbery of a bank in the vicinity, suggests that gangster crime may be developing.

Many of the police in Sardinia are from the mainland, and

Sards will never betray each other to a 'foreigner'. For the authorities, who realize to the full the necessity for stamping out these crimes, one of the greatest difficulties is this custom of *omerta*, the breaking of which could involve *vendetta alla morte*. At the time of the Scherer assault it was published in the papers that no less than twenty different people had seen the criminals, and that this time at least prompt arrest was likely to follow, must follow. Nothing happened.

Severe prison sentences of *banditi* who have been caught do not yet appear to have had very much effect in terms of the force of example. Nor do prison bars always hold their *malviventi* in Sardinia, any more than in other countries, even when they are caught and convicted. What undoubtedly hampers the police considerably is this loyalty to friend, family or clan that has for hundreds of years often meant survival in the face of savage butchery, or to a simple, proud and fundamentally honest people, what might seem worse—slavery in a foreign land. It is an ingrained habit, as natural as sleeping and eating, and as basic, the results of failure to observe it in the past being so dire that only blood could wash away the stain. I heard it said more than once that if a Sard is your friend he is your friend for life.

Severe punitive measures, though they might succeed in the end, could possibly meanwhile, therefore, breed still more bitterness, and perhaps for a short time even greater resistance among a certain section of the people. There are caves and forests in the island where fugitives could hide for a long time, some of the former known only to *fuorilegge*. Obviously some means have got to be found to persuade the *Sardi* to stop slaughtering and kidnapping each other, but authorities who know the Sards well do not think this will be achieved either easily or quickly. It will, in any case, involve the acceptance of a whole change of values among the people themselves. The real answer, of course, lies in the development of two things: in education and better living conditions; in decent work which would enable a man to keep his self-respect and at the same time provide more amenities for himself and his family.

Adding, perhaps, to the difficulties of this complex situation, is the comparatively sudden influx of extreme wealth and luxury in the development of the *Costa Smeralda*, in what hitherto has been one of the poorest regions. Projects, admirable in themselves and eventually good for the whole island, but possibly at first representing too much, too quickly, too soon to be absorbed immediately in their proper perspective without difficulty.

*   *   *

Back in Nuoro, Aurelio Simonassi, the manager of the Jolly, a pleasant and helpful Italian from Bari, met me at the door and enquired if I had had a good day. Where had I been this time? 'To Orgosolo.' He gave a wry smile. 'It seems that journalists are not very lucky there at the moment!' I laughed and said I had good friends there and was returning the next day for the *festa*.

Later, in the restaurant, the Neapolitan *maître d'hôtel*, Nicola —'It is a Russian name, *signora*, but I am not Russian,' with a little deprecatory shrug—Nicola, too, as usual, asked where I had been, and if I had enjoyed my long day. I said I had had a marvellous time, in Orgosolo. '*Ma, signora!*' The round, pale face, the dark, velvet eyes grew troubled. He nearly dropped his order pad. I reassured him, saying I had friends who took good care of me. 'But you were all by yourself on the road.' He was the kindest of men, taking great trouble to see that nice things were sent to me when I was laid up for a couple of days. Among the many Jolly hotels in which I have stayed this one, in fact, had much the best menu, including local dishes and a greater variety than is usual in these *alberghi*. The chef, too, was Neapolitan, as severely lean and handsome as Nicola was round. Through the plate glass window dividing his domain from the rest of us he ruled, crowned with that tall, dazzlingly white hat, and his bow, indicating good morning, or good evening as the case might be, was a masterpiece of dignity, though he also had a wicked twinkle. Giuseppi, my waiter, was good value, too. He was learning English prior to stepping out into the big world, and practised on me. 'Naif,' he would say, firmly planting a knife in front of me. 'Glass,' 'plate,' 'beeg plate', and so on. Before I left we had nearly got to sentences.

By the time I set out for Orgosolo the next day I had made up my mind to carry on as I had originally intended, rather than quit the region and go south, which was the only real alternative. I very much wanted to see Sorgono and Desulo, as well as something of the Gennargentu itself at close quarters, however briefly. This wasn't casting myself in any sort of heroic role at all, and I did occasionally have the feeling of a slightly chilly draught down my spine driving along the empty, winding roads, but I hoped that *fuorilegge* planning any further assaults were deciding to lie doggo for the time being in view of the publicity being given to the unfortunate Cristopher Scherer. I had tried quietly to consider what to do if I should be held up and decided I hadn't the slightest idea of what my reactions would be. I only hoped I wouldn't panic. Once before, many years ago, I had found myself looking down the wrong end of a gun and had no wish at all to repeat that experience.

More than that all was to chance, so I stopped cogitating and gave myself up to the more pleasant considerations of the moment, and felt better for putting imponderables behind me.

The streets and alleyways of Orgosolo were full of people this time, mostly men, only the older ones in the traditional black and white dress. Others were in ordinary suits with tieless shirts mostly closed at the neck, and wearing caps on their heads. Driving quietly through the crowd I made for the place to which I had been directed by the Grey Man of yesterday, and amid some hard stares tucked the car in there well out of the way. I was getting my cameras out of the car when two men passed on either side of the vehicle to the extreme corners of the niche, to the accompaniment of some ribaldry in *Sardo*, and I realized what the nook was used for in emergencies. Obviously the only thing to do was to ignore this, so when I was ready I got out, locked the door and walked through the knot of men as though nothing had happened. I was pretty sure this wouldn't have occurred if Gianetto had been there, and sought the café which was to be the rendezvous with the two Marios. They were not ʇɹɐ ʇǝʎᴉʌǝɹ, so feeling it would be well to establish some sort of standing without delay I turned to a bunch of men and asked if anyone knew of the whereabouts of Mario Tomainu or Mario Mattana, whom I was to meet there. At once the atmosphere changed, a couple of men promptly replied they would find them, for which I thanked them and said I would be continuing down the street.

Within moments two young figures were smiling a welcome behind me, Mario Tomainu, gay, handsome, quicksilver; Mario Mattana quieter, a gentle sensitivity governing his manner and large, expressive hazel eyes, partly explained perhaps by that slight limp. They said the *cavalcata* would be held later in the main street, and asked if meanwhile I would like to see an Orgosolo costume, for which they took me round narrow lanes to Mario Mattana's grandfather's house. The old man himself, in the magpie dress, was outside, being photographed by a French couple who happened to be passing through at this auspicious moment. Sitting on a corner stone the grandmother watched passers-by with an inscrutable expression on a marvellous face, worn now, with the stresses of life, heavy, malarial, but those dark, steady eyes had seen so much, missed so little. It was a face of courage and dignity, and acceptance.

We were all taken into the house, regaled with *vernaccia*, some local liqueur, and macaroons, and shown the costumes being expertly made by two elderly aunts. A man's coat for Mario's brother of fine scarlet cloth with bright blue facings and insets, all held with gold braiding, the slit sleeves and lapels also gold braided, was a beautiful and expert piece of work, as was the beginnings of a girl's costume, an apron exquisitely embroidered and appliqued in a design of many colours. What was completed so far obviously represented weeks of skilled labour, the finished garments would be quite outstanding.

Word was brought that the *cavalcata* was assembling, so down we went to the thronged main street. On the way a large double gate in an apparently blank wall was opened to reveal one of those hidden, flower-filled courtyards, on this occasion crowded also with the family clustering round a fine chestnut horse, already saddled and being garlanded in addition with a narrow collar worked with brightly-coloured wools and ringed with bells. The horse took the attention very calmly, shook his bells and nuzzled at my hand expectantly.

Village girls in small groups were weaving in and out, arm in arm, a few older women were in the background, but lining the way on either side were the men of Orgosolo, a solid, shifting phalanx. On average they were taller than I had expected, proud vigour in their stride and in their faces, a vigour that probably would brook little opposition, real or otherwise. At the moment, however, they were cheerful and peaceful enough, obviously exchanging news and tossing jokes back and forth, appraising the horses and their riders now gathering in a small open space on a rise just above us. Boys and older men were perched on every available ledge.

The horses looked in good condition with bright eyes, ears well forward and shining coats, their tails bound, each bearing his gaily-worked collar of bells. One of the riders on a big grey, very smart in black and white checked breeches, carried a small banner, the carnival insignia, and suddenly the first pair were away. The display was in the manner of the Cagliari *pareggia*, where riders start together with outstretched arms interlocked and held at shoulder level, the merit being to arrive at the finish, galloping flat out, still holding together. In Cagliari at one time they rode as many as six abreast, but the sport proved so dangerous that eventually this number was reduced by regulation.

Here, in Orgosolo, the men rode in pairs, clattering full stretch down the hard, dusty village street as if it had been good turf. When all had made their original gallop the return journey was ridden in the same way, not many arriving in the linked manner of their start, and horsemanship varying considerably in terms of style. One man on a big bay apparently felt the only way to stop his horse was to lie almost flat on his back. How he stayed on was a mystery of muscle and balance, particularly as on the return trip he had lost a stirrup, and judging by the expression on his face he wasn't quite clear either how he had achieved the miracle. It was an astonishing performance. But everybody was happy.

After the dust had settled and all concerned had had time to recover breath the horsemen set out in sober order for the *parrochia*. There are nine other churches in Orgosolo, and an eleventh is being built, but this was the principal one. Quicksilver Mario Tomainu had disappeared in great excitement with one of my cameras, and in fact took some very good pictures. Mario Mattana, gentle and charming, was still with me, so together we went under the bridge spanning the street, down an uneven cobbled lane to the church. By the time we arrived the horses were already settled in a quiet semicircle facing the main door, and in the interim, through the browband of each animal had been thrust a plume of green leaves. The service was still in progress and for the most part they waited patiently enough, only one or two of the horsemen or their mounts becoming restless. These had a private gallop of their own round the building, returning to their places in the line without sign or comment from their friends. By this time it was nearly 6.30, the light was beginning to fade from the sky.

After what seemed a long wait the church doors were opened, worshippers emerged to sort themselves out and a long procession began to take shape. Led by the horsemen, now four abreast riding with quiet discipline, the cavalcade began its journey past the churchyard, up the hill, to wind through the village.

Behind the horsemen a little knot of children clad in their Sunday best walked demurely hand in hand, some obviously conscious of the importance of this moment, others finding it difficult not to look around to see if their friends and relatives were observing them. Following came a long double file of women, with a wide gap between the two ranks, in the centre of which were six more women carrying aloft gold and white banners emblazoned with emblems representing the saint and symbols associated with him. All these women were dressed alike in long, fringed, dark brown shawls of fine wool that enveloped them completely, each held closely at the throat by a gold filagree brooch. On their heads a small, fringed shawl of similar colour and texture was drawn forward shading their brows, and, as is customary in the area, was wrapped across throat and chin, possibly an inheritance from long-ago Arab penetration. Behind them came a few nuns and two older women in the pride of their full Orgosolo costume, the pleated skirt this time ablaze with a scarlet-edged emerald green moiré band, sleeves and aggressively jutting lapels of small, tight boleros also embellished with scarlet, though on this occasion their aprons were dark and plain, unlike the beautifully embroidered version we had seen in the Mattana household.

Now came choir boys, leading the priest clad in a great sweeping cope of brilliant violet silk lavishly embroidered with vivid yellow and gold. At the end of the line a handful of men in ordinary clothes brought up the rear.

As the last man disappeared round the curve of the road to turn into the main thoroughfare Mario Mattana and I hurried back to take up a position in a doorway in the centre of the village, in the midst of a group of waiting men. The procession came slowly into view, conversation ceased, those who had been taking their ease on doorsteps rose, men took off their caps. The only sounds to be heard were the quiet clip-clop of the horses' hooves as they moved gently forward, and the low voices of the women rising and falling in rhythmic cadences murmuring responses to the invocations intoned by the priest.

In this place of fierce loyalties, of sudden violence, and many secrets, this long, slow file of half-hidden brown women, rosaries in their hands—the whole thing—had an air of medieval mystique, of translation to some other age and sphere that epitomised all one had heard, learned and felt about these mountain villages. In a way it somehow made them seem oddly defenceless against the onslaught of modern pressures knocking at their doors, in spite of all their pride and courage, or perhaps because of it.

We were shortly joined by Mario Tomainu, and very soon after I took reluctant leave of my two good cavaliers. The village was agog, and likely to become more so I thought, but the time had come to go.

*   *   *

At the Jolly there was a message from Nicolino Porcu wanting to know when I would visit Serra Orrios, the site of one of the most important nuraghic villages in Sardinia, on the road to Dorgali.

So, on Saturday, my last day in Nuoro, I set out early for the trip. As on my previous visit it was a day of blazing sunshine, not a flicker of wind stirred the leaves, under the ancient olive tree the same flock of sheep stood congealed. In the brilliant light Oliena shimmered even more than usual in a blue haze; behind, Monte Orgosolo rose, sombre, greener, darker. The vines were neatly trimmed in the chocolate earth, and as I passed the same two men were mending the old, dry stone wall where I had photographed the bullock cart. They called: '*Buon giorno, signora, va bene?*' I waved. '*Va bene, grazie.*'

Nicolino Porcu was waiting for me, as spruce as ever, and as courteous, but with a difference somehow behind those dark glasses. We set out, first of all for Cala Gonone again, where there were also important nuraghic remains, and gradually the sad fact emerged. Nicolino had a hangover. A very bad hangover. It was the result of a party on the previous evening to celebrate the purchase by a friend of a new, white, low-slung car, a very fast sports model. 'Did you mix your drinks?' I asked. '*Sì.*' 'Oh, dear. All right, I'll drive.' Previously I had yielded the wheel to Nicolino in deference to his masculine ego, and that *brutta figura* business. Sard men don't like women to seem to be taking the initiative, but now he subsided thankfully into the passenger seat.

At Cala Gonone his friend of our previous visit was waiting to act as guide, but though we did a good deal of scrambling over rough ground there was little really of great interest here, except perhaps for knowledgeable archaeologists. But Nicolino was conscientiously determined that I should see everything possible. So we next went on to explore a new road being built right along the coast. Still in the elementary stage it was nevertheless very impressive. High above small white bays enclosing innumerable grottos invisible to us then from our lofty position we looked down on the transparent water. Northward, in the distance, a stretch of pale sand marked Orosei itself, still further, near Siniscola, Capo Comino reached a long, white arm far out into the sea. Southward, to the Capo di Monte Santu, the same tranquil scene was laid out, miles and miles of it, with never a human in sight. But hangover or not, Nicolino and his companion would stand nonchalantly on the edge of this road sheer over the beaches, or sit with legs dangling, and for I, who suffer from vertigo, it was paralysing to see them, to look down that 500 feet drop.

The very thought of lunch made Nicolino shudder, so once again I ate delicious lobster alone, and afterwards, while a midday silence hung in the calm air, lay full-length watching the sea change colour to an infinitely far horizon.

Serra Orrios lies about midway between Nuoro and Dorgali, and as we passed again through the latter I asked about the frequent Communist slogans on walls. Were there many Communists hereabouts? 'Yes, in theory. But they really don't know what it is all about.' It was the same answer I had received elsewhere. After all for those who have next to nothing the idea of fair shares for everyone is very attractive; it is only later that disillusion sets in.

Passing the river Cedrino we turned sharply to the right through a gateway, and for a short distance followed a rough track through farmland. Dry stone walls and prickly pear hedges bordered olive groves, underfoot corn stubble was harsh and dry. There was nothing to indicate the whereabouts of the village site, but as we wandered we were suddenly confronted by a very small man indeed who asked if we were looking for the *nuraghe* village. To which he led us, through several more fields and to a slight rise.

Small and grizzled, Giovanni Carta had been *pastore* on this farm since 1925. He could neither read nor write—'but I can count my sheep,' he confided with an impish grin. As he led us forward the usual questions flowed, with one or two additions this time. 'Where do you come from? Why are you alone?' When I replied that I was a widow Giovanni looked at me quickly. 'Then why don't you wear a black dress like our widows?' He looked again. 'You are wearing blue trousers.' I suggested that apart from the fact that widows in my country were not expected, as were those in Sardinia, to wear mourning for the rest of their lives, that trousers were more convenient for such travelling as I was doing, and for the taking of photographs that sometimes involved climbing walls, which he had, indeed, just helped me to do. He nodded, agreeing that this was more convenient, then demanded, with a chuckle: 'How old are you? I'm sure I'm older than you.' I replied that I had a grown-up son, which at first he gallantly refused to believe possible. But that at least established my right to be considered as a human being of some achievement. Not to have had a son, and to be a widow, would have rendered me as of little worth, as I well knew.

Just as we came upon the *nuraghe* village a pair of turtle doves glided down from the branch of a tree to the ground near us. Giovanni's face softened into an affectionate smile. 'I like those little birds, they know me,' he said, and stood watching them for several seconds.

Here, half covered by grass and bushes, is the remains of a large village thought to date back to about the sixth or seventh century B.C. According to Giovanni, who obviously took great pride in his guardianship, some seventy buildings had already been identified, together with a *piazza*, streets, two temples, and two wells; one of these last still with water in it, that legend suggests has never failed. Another thirty buildings, at least, are understood to be beneath the undergrowth, yet to be excavated.

In one of the temples an important bronze figure was found, now lodged in the Cagliari museum. The heavy, curved architrave over the entrance to this building still stands as firmly as ever. Within easy distance also is a defensive *nuraghe*, thought to have been used as a shelter in times of war. And what was not apparent at first was the commanding position of the site that takes in a 360 degrees sweep across miles of wild, rocky *macchia* to the distant mountains.

Under the blazing sun Giovanni led me scrambling all over the place, but eventually even I had had enough, and the little man asked if we would like a drink of water. 'Yes, please,' we said as one. So he took us to his home a short distance across the fields. In front of the long single-storey building two huge, sleek bullocks, one cream-coloured, the other a golden tan, were treading an endless, circular path round and round over bean-stalks, crushing out the seed for winter feed. I wondered if the man walking behind, guiding the animals with a long rein on their slow path, ever needed to go into reverse to stop being mesmerised by this incessant one-way circling. But no, it seemed he didn't mind it.

Giovanni's wife, hearing voices, came to the door. A little, plump, rosy-cheeked robin of a woman, dressed in a long black skirt, printed blouse, and a small, square cap on her neat hair, she appeared in the doorway distaff in hand, spinning uncon-cernedly as she greeted us with a beaming smile. Glasses were produced and delicious, cold, sparkling water was poured from a beautiful, narrow necked terracotta pitcher standing on the stone floor at one side of the door as we entered. This was the living room, fairly lofty under the eaves and a good size, with a large table in the centre, a cupboard on the right wall, and opposite the door, by a window, a butane gas cooker on some sort of metal stand. A smaller table, washing up apparatus, and a dresser, together with chairs and a couple of prints completed the furnishings. To the left, leading out of this room, was the store, and to the right, the bedroom into which Giovanni's wife disappeared to return with a sock to show us, expertly knitted for her husband of the natural wool such as she was spinning. They were obviously happy, proud of each other, utterly unself-conscious, with an ease of manner that was once more a delight to meet. Waving goodbye from the doorway they bade us come back soon.

The sequel was equally pleasant. Returning to London I presently sent prints of some of the pictures I had taken of them and of the farm. Immediately they wrote delighted acknow-ledgement, hoping 'with all their hearts' that I would come again many times to Sardinia, and that I would find great happiness there.

Part Four

*

THE GENNARGENTU

After breakfast on Sunday morning I turned the car south-wards, making for Aritzo via Fonni and Desulo. Accommodation of any kind is very limited in the region and I had been advised that the Albergo Moderno at Aritzo would be the best point from which to visit Sorgono, castigated so severely by Lawrence.

The route lay again through Mamoiada, past the dry *macchia*, the cork oaks, the *nuraghe*. In the village a row of men sat on the church steps dressed in their Sunday best; the women were obviously still about their household chores. A delicious smell of woodsmoke hung in the air.

About a mile beyond the village, round a sharp bend in the narrow road, a whole race of pigs, large and small, were wandering all over the lane. Yards behind the main bulk of the grunting, weaving mass came the smallest runt, complaining loudly, and far behind that the youthful *pastore* strolled placidly, apparently with not a care in the world. A short distance further on I was able to warn an oncoming car. The driver slowed down, calling as he passed: 'Thank you, *signora*. I don't like freshly killed meat!'

Terracing marks the rising steepness of the land, and soon after began the climb to Fonni, the highest village in Sardinia some 3,300 feet, on the slopes of Monte Spada, but in its isolation feeling much higher. Once again here was the dense and lovely border of roadside flowers, the blackberry blossom, but now, more and more the dark of evergreen oaks gave place to the lighter green of sweet chestnut trees, at this period almost smothered with plumes of scented creamy-yellow blossom, the pollen a pale cloud if a branch was touched. Every turn in the road offered a new prospect across mountain and valley. I pulled up and got out to stand on the top of a grassy bank. In the golden sunshine the blue sky seemed higher than ever, the only sounds to break the silence the murmur of bees, the singing of small birds.

Within sight of Fonni, southward and slightly to the east, the highest peaks began to be visible. Tucked into a shelf of the mountain near the road a small farm broke the line of forest and outcrop with ripe corn, a few acres of vines, and a marvellously bright green patch that looked to be some sort of vegetable.

Fonni itself was enjoying Sabbath calm. It is a grey stone village with a grim reputation for savage vengeance among the *Sardi* themselves, but a local tag: 'Never spend a night in Fonni,' is not intended in connection with assassination. Rather it has to do with comfort. Unfortunately I had missed the annual carnival that takes place on the first Sunday in June, said to be a splendid affair, with displays of horsemanship at which the men excel. Somewhat ironically, it might be felt, it is the Feast of the Martyrs that is celebrated, though this, one is assured, does not relate to local inhabitants.

Beyond the village tall poplars marked the track of a stream. Up the hill came a man on a big grey mare followed by its young foal, also grey, a pretty thing that nuzzled softly at my hand to the astonishment, I sensed, but not to the pleasure of the rider, a burly, tough-looking character. Perhaps once again it was my trousers that offended, and on a Sunday at that. Anyhow, and unusually, he gave no reply to my '*buon giorno*' as I stroked the little foal's neck. So we went our different ways without more ado.

As the road led upwards curves became sharper, valleys narrower, peaks steeper, red stonecrop clinging to shale gleaming in the sunlight where the road had been cut through sheer rock. Once or twice, bedded down in sheltered nooks, were tiny stone huts of shepherds or woodcutters, each in turn marked by one of those patches of vivid green.

On what proved to be nearly the highest point of the road I

stopped again and got out the better to see this unbelievable panorama. Further than ever, layer on shimmering layer the mountains receded into the distance. It seemed impossible that the island really could be so comparatively small. Now Sardinia's two topmost peaks were visible, the Bruncu Spina, and La Marmora, the former just under, the latter just over 6,000 feet, both thickly wooded, greener than I had expected. and from the heights of either of which can be seen the soft line of the sea on both east and west coasts.

In these forests, along with the more common fox and boar, are to be found the rarer wild cats, marten, fallow deer and the shy herds of *muffloni*; vultures soar, on remote crags eagles nest, underfoot are orchids among an abundance of other flowers.

I have not yet seen the Gennargnetu—the Silver Gate—in winter, so named for the reflection of the sun on the snows. But there is no real basis of comparison between these rolling heights and the icy grandeur of the more lofty Italian alps with their deep, cosy valleys, or with Etna. The Gennargentu country has a powerful *ambiente* entirely its own, quite different—a wild, magnetic vitality to be discovered by each traveller for himself. Few who venture remain unmoved by it.

On this summer day butterflies like patchwork gauze fluttered in fragile clusters over the myriad blossoms, and particularly round a single thistle plant full of aggressive purple flowering, standing sentinel on a little knoll. The air was cooler here, with a marvellous freshness, birds were singing—one, with a phrase always ending on a single, clear, high note, repeated his call again and again for several minutes. An occasional wisp of white cloud drifted low on the horizon.

Suddenly feeling myself not alone I turned my head to find a woman squatting motionless in the shade of a tree at the edge of a sheer drop. Piercing dark eyes were watching me intently, and for a few seconds she remained without moving, only the glittering blackberry eyes alive. Then she rose to her feet and came towards me. She was dressed in the scarlet costume of Desulo, faded and worn this time, but still brilliant, and under the red bolero her white cotton blouse was pristine. Thick, wavy grey hair was uncovered, which was unusual, but I imagined she had perhaps taken off her kerchief while resting under the tree. Still with that fierce gaze on my face she demanded: 'What are you doing here?' I told her I was going to Aritzo. 'Why are you alone?' I replied, truly, that I had left friends in Nuoro, that others were awaiting me in the south. She grunted and moved across, peering into the car. 'You've a lot of luggage. What about giving me a lift?' I said that much as I would have liked to my insurance prohibited this.

The previous year, in Calabria, I had been warned never to give a lift to anyone in Italy because in the event of the slightest accident involving a third party, no matter how innocent of offence one might be, legal complications just went on and on interminably. Occasionally I had felt very mean about this, but mistrust of the possible consequences had kept me hard-hearted.

I asked where my questioner herself lived. 'Oh, over there,' with a vague wave of the arm, so, after a few more pressing enquiries on her part, and replies in vague generalities on mine, I got back into the car and we parted with mutual smiles and waves.

The road, a *strada bianca*, was being repaired some miles further on, and as I eased gently round a sharp bend by a glistening mound of shale, there, laid out beneath the sheltering edge of a steep slope, lay Desulo, high above a narrow valley at the bottom of which a glint of water was visible through the trees. Opposite, in the distance, rose La Marmora.

I drove slowly into the village, past the church from which an elderly priest, leaning out of a window of the bell tower, raised a hand in greeting. Alongside the petrol pump I stopped, not only for supplies, but because I had found that this was the man, always friendly and helpful, who was invariably a mine of information. This one was true to pattern. Today the feast of San Sebastiano was being celebrated, there would be a procession later in the afternoon, why not go on to Aritzo now, and return after lunch, he suggested. There would be more doing then. It sounded a good idea, so on I went, the serpentine road winding round and round, down, and then, following a sharp

Taking the bark from a cork tree

The procession at Orgosolo—Festa di San Pietro, and (*right*) Façade of Cagliari cathedral

On the road to Macomer—a small *nuraghe* sentinel on the hill

The same road, from the other side, with mountains in the distance

The Pisan Basilica di Santa Trinità di Saccargia—Sassari

turn, up again. Belvi, bunched on a bend, consisted of tiny houses some colour-washed pale pink or blue, roadside and garden flowers mingling around them, and hanging over stone walls. There were sweet peas, roses, several varieties of vetch, broom, white flowers, blue and yellow; cistus was in bloom and, inevitably, the blackberry.

A short distance and another turn led into Aritzo, a scatter of houses either side of a steep hill. Nearly at the top a sign indicated the Albergo Moderno, opposite an old stone wall over which roses were trailing and hollyhocks nodded. The *Moderno* part was correct in that there was running water, and a private bathroom, but sad to relate, though the bed was spotless, the rest of the room was not so. Food and service both proved indifferent, to the annoyance of several other travellers who had stopped here for their Sunday midday meal.

We were waited on by a couple of lads whose apparent lack of skill, and in one case of wits, was balanced by their obvious desire to please. No one had any quarrel with them, but food was very slow in coming and not well cooked.

At dinner time the simple lad was all on his own, carrying plates on the flat of his hand, never more than one at a time, so carefully it was almost painful to watch his agony of fear that he might drop the thing. In the evening he appeared clad in a spotless new white cotton vest with the numerals 007 embroidered on the pocket. Slow in the uptake, thinking this might have some significance in connection with perhaps local sport, or a club, and wanting to encourage him I asked what the numbers referred to. He gazed at me pityingly, rooted in his tracks by such extraordinary ignorance. 'But, *signora*, this is Bond, 007!'

Shortly afterwards Parry's music set to William Blake's hymn *Jerusalem* wheezed out from an agonized record player of some sort, a combination almost too good to be true.

My friend at the petrol pump had been right, Desulo was full of comings and goings later in the afternoon. The village is long and narrow, so much so that nearly all the houses are on one side of the main street, the land dropping away steeply opposite.

And what was puzzling was that at one end of the village fairy lights strung across the road, several stalls selling sweetmeats and knick-knacks, and a rifle range already being patronized, had the proper elements of a *festa*, while at the other end the *parrochia* bell was tolling. Which seemed strange pairing, even for a Sunday. I asked if this was usual on such occasions, to be given the unhappy news that the bell was for the funeral of a lad of only sixteen who had been accidentally killed by a fall from some rocky place. Sure enough, very soon the cortège began its sad passage. The pathetically small coffin, covered with wreaths and flowers, was followed by ten cars full of men, only men as this was a male death. In the front vehicle rode the desolate father weeping for his firstborn. Some distance behind women in their scarlet costumes passed in groups of two or three on foot, presumably also going to the church as they wore long black veils. Fitting their heads like monks' cowls these swept backwards in pleats to a point at the back held at hip level with a small bow. In front long streamers which the wearers held were presumably useful when winds were fierce. I kept quietly in the background, longing to take pictures of the women, but fearing to intrude on such an occasion. I was leaning against a stone wall beneath a row of terraced cottages. Over the portico of the nearest a splendid vine had been trained and obviously carefully tended, bunches of grapes looked well shaped and were already filling out. In front of the door sat a very small elderly man with clear-cut features and bright eyes who was watching me closely, so presently I bade him good afternoon, and to start the conversation commented on his beautiful vine, which obviously pleased him.

He said the dead boy was an only son, shaking his grey head in sympathy. I suggested that the gaieties at one end of the village and a funeral at the other was not a very happy mixture, which he explained with an interesting piece of local history. Desulo, he said, had originally been three separate communities started by three different families, one of whom bred cattle, another, sheep, the third, pigs. In the course of time the settlements had developed, encroaching upon each other, so that now it seemed as if there was but one village, whereas there were still three distinct groups, and the original names, of a language today unknown, neither *Sardo* nor any other recognizable tongue, were Isiria, Asuai and Ovolaccio. By a lucky chance I was able to confirm this information later in Cagliari, as far as the names were concerned, so presumably the rest of the story is correct. And yet again unanswerable questions suggested themselves.

This must have been a migration carefully planned. Where had these wanderers come from? What disaster, what threat had caused the three families together to seek refuge and finally settle in this remote, secret place? It was well chosen. Even nowadays Desulo is not visible until one is almost on it, and that only by the grace of a good, modern road.

Down at the *benzina* pump again I asked the attendant if I might take a photograph of his wife, a sweetly pretty creature with lovely eyes. Yes, certainly, he said. But would I please not make her laugh as she had just had her teeth out and was very self-conscious about it. She smiled ravishingly with her eyes, anyhow, so that was enough. I also asked about the strange ruin of a house in the heart of the village, but he said he knew nothing of its history, and inhibited by the funeral that would soon pass again on its way to the cemetery among the merrymakers at the other end of the village, I didn't feel it would be politic to pursue enquiries. Strangers asking questions are never popular in these villages of closed communities, at that moment even to have taken pictures of the mysterious house would have made me definitely unwelcome, of that I was sure. I had already observed some other than friendly looks from one or two of the older women, and it takes time to establish an easy relationship. Opportunities at this moment were limited, as they had been at Orgosolo, which was just unlucky.

A two-storey building of grey stone, the house was comparatively large, possibly early eighteenth century, I thought. It was entered from an imposing flight of stone steps, now broken and weed-grown; windows either side of the door were well proportioned, on a parapet over the stone porch life-size eagles, expertly carved with wings spread, were worn by wind and rain. The

house was like a sad, blind face set above the constant passing
of the villagers. How had a mansion of this size come to be built
in such a place, what had led to its abandonment, to the downfall presumably, or death of the family who had once been its
proud owners?

Owing to the funeral I gathered the procession I had hoped
to see had been abandoned, so, regretfully, I returned to Aritzo.
According to Tyndale the old name for this village had been
Genne-a-entu, Gate of the Wind, and certainly from an important road junction at the top of the hill the view boxed the
compass. Obviously it would be a stormy height in winter, but
at this moment the breeze was gentler, and from the crossroads
there was an unrivalled sight of an amazing sunset in lurid
picture postcard colourings. Gallura, Sassari, Nuoro, now the
Gennargentu, and later, Cagliari, each had its own special
brand of glorious sunsets. Only in this area were they quite so
fiery.

A noisy and prolonged altercation in the kitchen that evening
caused long delays when it came to dinner, and the patience of
some dozen hungry guests, mostly men and obviously habitués,
was distinctly ruffled by the time the first course made its appearance. It was the preface to a disturbed night, screams in the
village at two in the morning suggesting nothing less than bloody
murder, though later enquiries revealed no more than a con-
vivial family celebration, but one the local *carabinieri* had
eventually been called by local residents to subdue. It was enough
also to agitate a donkey in an adjoining field. His hoarse protests
continued on and off for the rest of the night.

The next morning my breakfast was nearly an hour late, and
when it arrived there was no butter, the coffee was nearly cold
and there was skin on the milk. The wife of the *padrone* brought
it. 'Scusi, signora.' The dark eyes were pleading. Still young, with
the remains of a soft, magnolia beauty, she had a defeated, unhappy look that explained much, and the reason was not far to
seek.

A little later I was settling myself in the car prior to going to
Sorgono when the *padrone* himself came rushing from the back

entrance. A tiny, surly, black-visaged man, he accused me: 'Where are you going? Your bill isn't paid?' I replied that I was coming back that evening. 'How do I know?' 'Because all my luggage is upstairs. Perhaps you would like to go and see, I will wait,' I suggested mildly. But he wasn't mollified, and ambled off, muttering. Obviously three suitcases against one night's lodging were quite inadequate.

To Sorgono the way led through Belvi and Tonara, the road cut through dense mountain slopes, girdled with more chestnuts, their pale flower fronds gilded by the morning sun. There were walnut trees, too, laden with a profusion of nuts in their green sheaths. *Pastori* were on the move with herds of sheep whose bells tinkled on all sides.

Tonara sits on a rounded hilltop, visible from a long way off, mostly apricot-coloured in the distance, close-to its walls plastered with slogans such as 'People why don't you wake up?' Around the village and the rest of the way to Sorgono shallower valleys were highly cultivated, mostly with corn, vines and fruit trees. In one place men were cutting ripe barley with a sickle.

Some miles past Tonara inadequate signposts left me baffled and I stopped a couple of road police on their motor cycles to ask which was the right turning. 'We'll show you,' they volunteered, saying they were in any case going that way. 'But you travel a lot faster than I do,' I suggested, having seen many of their kind streaking along. They laughed. 'You're wise. These roads are very dangerous.' And they said they would go more slowly, so off we set in convoy, my police escort a few yards in front, going at a pretty good pace nonetheless. On the outskirts of Sorgono they indicated my route, peeling off with gay smiles and smart salutes.

Building was in progress in the village at either end, in one case of a school, the other a clinic for mothers and babies. I drove through, looking for the petrol pump; here the man said there was no *albergo* or *ristorante* called the *Risveglio*. He had never heard of it; there was only one *albergo*, his sister's, to which he directed me. It was alongside the *parrochia* and the bus stop where a few people were waiting. The 'pullman' arrived shortly but there were not many passengers this Monday morning.

In front of the church a cluster of men were chatting at the top of some steps leading to the inn in a narrow, lower lane. I parked the car in the shade of a big walnut tree to the accompaniment of familiar, curious stares and strolled off to explore. Little groups of men were standing about as though with time on their hands; only at the building sites were there signs of real activity, but that again could have been shrouded by the ever-present plastic fringes masking open doors. There were the usual over-many café-bars. But round the corner from the main *piazza* pedlars with lorries had set out their wares. Fruit and vegetables were being inspected by intending purchasers and brisk business was being done. From two other vans clothes and textiles of various kinds had been laid out on the ground, carefully set on thick brown paper. These were attracting fewer customers, but round a sweet stall children clustered like bees round a honey pot.

Inside the church was an air of decay, tall columns led to a plain roof and there was nothing to suggest the usual village devotion to flowers real or imitation.

The *albergo* bar was empty, but after a few moments a pleasant-faced middle-aged woman appeared, in contrast to Lawrence's dirty, detested landlord of the Risveglio. Could I have lunch? 'Of course, *signora*,' she took me kindly by the hand and led me into a little inner room set with four tables. What would I like? We settled on *scallopina* and salad, with fruit to follow, which she disappeared to organize, and returning, sat beside me to chat, apparently glad to have a stranger to talk to. 'We don't have many travellers here.' Both she and her sister were unmarried, she confided, with a little despairing shrug, and as if to explain their unhappy state: 'There is only agriculture here, no industry, not enough work for the men. They go away.' I wanted to ask her if there were many other spinsters in Sorgono but thought it might hurt her feelings. Before I left she begged me to take a picture of the inn and send it to them. 'It might help business,' she and her sister hoped. In due course I sent it, doubtful of its efficacy as a provider of custom, but at least glad to have kept faith with them.

The photography broke the ice with the group of men I had originally seen at the top of the steps. They were still there, one of them with flaming, carroty hair, one of the very few redheads I saw anywhere in Sardinia. There were several children in the village with like colouring so it was obviously a family trait. I wondered at the origin.

We said good day to each other, question and answer following the usual pattern until, without warning, this was pushed beyond the general trivialities. Was I French? No, I was English. 'You don't speak Italian like English people.' Here, once more, was an ex-prisoner of war. I asked if they had many English travellers here. No, they said, never. In fact they rarely had any foreigners at all. A short, stocky greybeard looked at me accusingly. 'Why are you here? This is right in the middle of Sardinia, there is nothing interesting, no work, no sights to see, nothing, why have you come?' I explained that I was on my way south, from Gallura, and that forty-five years ago an Englishman had passed through Sorgono and mentioned it in a book he had written about his journey through the island. I was interested to see it, that was all. Did he like Sardinia, demanded one? I said, with truth, he thought the countryside was wonderful and that the men were *molto forti*, feeling pretty secure in the idea that they had not and would not read his uncomplimentary opinion of their village. 'Are you writing a book?' That caught me on the wrong foot. So far I had kept pretty quiet about my intentions. I could only say yes, I hoped to. At once interest quickened. Where had I been, what villages had I visited, how many Sards did I know personally? They pressed for details. From Nuoro where had I ranged? I told them '. . . and Orgosolo, where I have friends.' 'Ah': there was a deep murmur, then a tall, dark-haired man with fine, fair skin and grey eyes muttered: 'That was a bad business.' Greybeard quickly added: 'But they are very hospitable in Orgosolo. Don't you have *malviventi* in England? There are prisons there, too, aren't there?' I replied, yes, unfortunately we had both, as I thought did all countries. The answer satisfied them. But the old man wasn't finished. His look was direct, challenging: '*Signora*, aren't you afraid here, alone, sometimes?' Suddenly the waiting silence was tense. Five pairs of eyes bored into my face. The answer mattered to them, and I had a feeling they would see through insincerity. The answer mattered to me, too. 'Should I be?' I asked quietly. Greybeard thumped an emphatic fist into the other hand. '*No, no, no.*' The others grunted assent—'*Bene*'—and the tension was gone. They were content I should be among them, and their honour had been vindicated.

*   *   *

In Aritzo women were returning to their homes with the Monday washing in round plastic bowls on their heads, walking with that superb grace, full skirts swinging.

When I went into the Albergo Moderno the expression of sheer disbelief on the face of the *padrone* was comical. He obviously hadn't had any faith in those suitcases.

Part Five

*

CAGLIARI

Instead of going to Cagliari directly south, via Laconi, I had decided to take a longer route down the east coast, passing the Flumendosa dam at Villanova Strisaili, which meant retracing my steps through Desulo and turning right just before reaching Fonni.

At Belvi, two of the pedlars who had been at Sorgono the day before were laying out their goods on the same brown paper carpet spread over the road. No casual customers these, the women were examining garments and other possible purchases minutely, comparing notes amid general chaffing with the salesmen who appeared to take it as all part of a transaction, giving as good as they got by way of repartee.

In Desulo a number of women were again on their way to the church in their scarlet dresses, and wearing the long black veil. With most of the costumes I had seen, including some in the Nuoro museum, the short apron was generally of a different colour, for festive occasions often of lace; in Desulo it was of the red cloth of which the skirt was made, bordered with an appliqué of bright blue and yellow velvet. Sometimes it was worn as a cape, hanging straight down the back.

The pretty wife of the *benzina* man was at her post, and having filled my tank gave the windows an extra special polish.

It was a *strada bianca* all the way to Fonni, raising a lot of dust that made their long marches pretty disagreeable for the several shepherds on the way with their flocks of sheep or goats, but though nearly smothered by my dust as I passed, they took it in very good part.

The turn just before Fonni led to a first-class asphalted road, dropping through a *prato* in the centre of which ran a small stream bordered with poplars and walnuts. Baled hay or corn, stretches of pyrethrum in bloom, and vegetables now replaced oak, lower hills, either bare or covered with short turf, the previous wooden heights, while shale banks at the roadside were a mass of multi-coloured rock plants. On a hilltop in the distance stood a lone *nuraghe*.

Still descending, on a wide curve the way opened through a big gap cut into the hillside leading to lower, rolling lands; the sky was now overcast, and in place of the clear brilliance of the mountains the light was curiously flat and dead over the hills. At the bottom of an open valley cattle were herded within stone walls, an unusual sight.

Rain was beginning to fall by the time I arrived at the Albergo del Lago at Villanova Strisaili. Set in a bend of the main highway, it leads immediately to the straight stretch either side of which lie the houses and drab grey bungalows that constitute this neglected-looking village.

A pretty young girl appeared at the door as I mounted the steps, announced that she would collect my luggage and immediately went into action. I suggested that one at least of my suitcases was very heavy, perhaps there was a man who could carry it. 'Well, let me try,' was the cheerful reply, and forthwith she heaved the heavy case onto her head and walked steadily not only up these outside steps, but to the second floor of the building.

Promptly I was established in a large room with an excellent modern, newly installed bathroom, the whole spotlessly clean. A balcony gave an extensive view across the countryside.

The small dining-room was full for lunch, half the company obviously regulars, with their napkins in little cases, the rest, travellers like myself, were briefly *en route* for somewhere else. In addition to the men at two big tables, in the middle was a large family party of nine, across the room a married couple with the all too familiar spoilt child of about three or four, and next to me, a solitary man. In due course the *signora* herself appeared, a woman of enormous bulk, with a handsome intelligent face. She immediately demonstrated without the slightest fuss who ruled this establishment. The child, who had been running round unchecked in the usual way, was gently but firmly restored to his chair, much to his surprise. What was particularly fascinating was the way he understood authority immediately he met it; he cheerfully stayed put without a murmur for the rest of the meal. In no time at all everybody had decided what they would like from the menu and the *signora* disappeared to the kitchen regions.

In Sardinia, except in some of the first class hotels, generally the men carefully remove their jackets and hang them neatly on the chair back before sitting down to a meal. Here was an added quirk, coats were taken off, but caps were kept on.

Being a foreigner I was honoured, the plastic table cloth was changed in favour of a fresh cotton one, to which was added a little vase of flowers. I had chosen roast baby lamb, salad, cheese and fruit, none of which could have been bettered. '*Vino, signora?*' had queried my hostess, to whom I had replied that I would take whatever she recommended of the *vino da pasto*, the wine of the countryside. And delicious it was.

This sort of thing was repeated at every meal at the *albergo*. The food was simple but excellent, the *signora* a splendid cook and much of what was served was local produce. We were waited on by Nicolina, who had carried my luggage, and her elder sister, Carmela, the latter a beauty with pale face, regular features and enormous eyes fringed with unbelievable lashes. Dressed in black from head to toe, black kerchiefs on their young heads, black stockings beneath their knee-length black dresses and black felt slippers, they flitted back and forth like small, dark moths, noiseless, deft, quick, with ready smiles.

Later Carmela, who appeared to be in charge, showed me the stores. Neatly laid in a cool, stone lean-to, there must have been several hundred bottles of wine, apart from spirits and other drinks. Adjacent, in a long, narrow dark slip of a room great mountain hams hung in rows on the wall above a variety of sausages. On the floor, on a thick bed of thyme, were cheeses of several kinds ripening slowly in the dim coolness. In a far corner other herbs were piled, and by some clever arrangement of draught the rich air perfumed with this wealth of produce was fresh and pleasant, neither over-heated, nor over-powering. I asked Carmela if she found her job interesting, in reply to which she shrugged with that philosophic acceptance one had come to recognize. 'There is nothing else in this village.'

The rain had ceased by early afternoon so I went to look at the Flumendosa dam, an important source of water for Cagliari, and a project of which the Sards are very proud. The main supply comes from the seventy-six mile long Flumendosa river itself, rising in the extreme south of the Gennargentu between the Barbagia Belvi and the Barbagia Seulo; nearer Villanova Strisaili the dam is also fed by lesser streams. It is completely artificial, and to me drowned land always has a desolate, abandoned air. This was no exception. Much larger than Bidighinzu, near Sassari, irregularly shaped among low, containing hills, the level of the water at this time of year was not high. Under leaden skies it looked grey and heavy, utterly still—too still. At the edges charred tops of trees reached upward from their grave, and a broken stone pillar leaned in a despairing way. Reasonably enough the public is not allowed into the pumping station, but even the mass of water pouring into the gorge below seemed to have no light in it. I told myself that it was the weather that made it look so.

Returning to the *albergo* I picked some field flowers on the way and a couple of twigs from a bush covered with small, sweet-scented blossoms, setting the posy by my bedside.

*   *   *

Lanusei is a junction for Bari Sardo on the one side—on the main trunk road from the north to Cagliari—and on the other, for Tortoli and the much-praised red porphyry coast of Arbatax. The route between these two last had been described as the loneliest stretch in Sardinia. I couldn't think why when I traversed it next day.

Astonishing twists and turns of the road led to Lanusei piled high within sight of the sea. In the sunshine it proved to be a bustling little market town, the principal centre of the Ogliastra, a wine producing area, the famous Malmsey being one of its products, here known as *Malvasia*. Mixing with the men in business suits were solitary countrywomen, long-skirted, enveloped in their dark, fringed shawls, smaller ones on their heads drawn closely across throat and chin and sometimes over mouth as well. They strode on their way proudly erect, carefully covered baskets on their heads piled with fruit. Shops of all kinds appeared to be doing brisk business and the banks of Sardinia and of Naples had imposing premises on the main street. A general air of liveliness pervaded the whole place.

To Tortoli the road shot sharply down, gardens of private villas on the outskirts crowded with flowers bearing testimony to the richness of the soil. Through a considerable valley wound a river bed, huge clumps of bamboo and oleander mingling at its sandy edges; vineyards, orchards of peaches and apricots, fig trees, orange groves and banana palms flourished.

Tortoli itself had nothing of the bustle of Lanusei, and was something of an anticlimax. In the main *piazza* four enormous oleander trees were smothered with crimson blossom, looking like lovely red puff balls; on benches in front of this prodigality sat the sad row of old men, as usual. The flat road led along the salt marshes for miles, out to Capo Bellavista and Arbatax, towards long and lovely empty beaches of pink and white sand backed by rose-red rocks above the sparkling blue sea. But there was little development as yet for visitors.

* * *

I was leaving for Cagliari early next morning, so retired soon after dinner that evening to pack. In the process of rearranging a suitcase, out of the corner of my eye I saw a twig from my bedside posy drop forward. Turning, hand outstretched to set it straight, I stood transfixed. On the twig, the cause of its sudden movement, was the largest cricket I had ever seen, the very grandfather of a *grillo*, darkly speckled, its body a good three inches long. And if there is anything I really cannot abide indoors it is members of the insect world such as this, in particular in my bedroom, at night. Rigid, the *grillo* clung to the now still twig and we measured each other grimly. It was too big to trap into a glass, I had no suitable weapon, even my books were lying beside the flowers, and if I had thrown anything there was danger of hitting a little travelling clock also on the table. I moved slightly, to be met with an answering quiver. Which way would it leap?

At this moment I heard the voice of Nicolina in the passage and sped to the door. The room was L-shaped to accommodate the bathroom that had been carved out of the remaining quarter. At the door I called, Nicolina came at once. Certainly she would deal with the *grillo*, where was it? 'There,' I said, pointing. But there it was no longer. Nicolina searched, I searched, everywhere. At last she suggested very gently, as one coaxing a dangerous lunatic, that perhaps the *signora* had only *thought* she had seen it. Or perhaps it had escaped. The *signora* replied that she didn't imagine a *grillo* of that size, of any size, and how could it have escaped? Both shutters and windows were closed. The *signora* did not open them at night until the light was out. Moreover, I remembered that I had been awakened during the previous night by a blow in the face and had thought it was a moth. Obviously it was this horrible thing. The *grillo* was perhaps hiding under the bed, but wherever it was it had got to be found. So little Nicolina obediently got down on hands and knees to peer underneath. It wasn't there. She looked at me in desperation. '*Momento, signora, momento.*' She ran to the door. I followed more slowly to see where she was going, glancing into the bathroom as I passed. On the bath sat the *grillo*, looking balefully around. I hastily closed the door. In a few moments Nicolina was back with a stout, fan-shaped broom, and another of the girls who worked in the kitchen. I pointed to the bathroom and said there was the quarry. '*Nel bagno?*' queried Nicolina a little doubtfully, but opening the door they saw it, and armed with their weapon went in to do battle, closing the door behind them. I retreated to the furthest corner of the bedroom and listened to the crashing and banging that ensued. Presently the door was reopened and the girls appeared, Nicolina pushing the corpse along with the broom. '*Scusi, signora.*' She looked at me appealingly. Yes, it was a very large *grillo*, of a type that only came out at night, the *signora* had been quite correct. Now she hoped all would be well and that I would sleep peacefully. With mutual good-nights and my thanks, they left.

I finished packing, went to bed, still a little uneasy, lay reading for a short time and eventually put out the light.

From a sound sleep I was awakened by a smart blow on my right ear. Instinctively I knew this was another *grillo*. Moving only my left arm I reached very slowly and carefully for the switch and, the lights on, turned my head equally cautiously in the opposite direction, to the side from which the blow had come. This was a large double bed. On the other pillow, not two feet from my face was a second, enormous *grillo*, gazing at me with an indignant, basilisk stare, poised, ready to spring. In what direction? It was two o'clock in the morning. This time there would be no escape, I was quite alone. After a few paralysed seconds, slowly, carefully, I edged my way off the bed, keeping watch on the creature all the time. A slight flicker of the eyes showed, in its turn, how aware it was of my movements. Gently I slid to the ground, thrust my feet into slippers, picking up a book as I did so, and waited. So did the *grillo*. We both went on waiting. Then I hurled the book—and missed. Or perhaps the brute had moved a fraction of a second quicker. Anyhow, there it was, now on the bedhead, still glowering at me. But at least it was against a solid background. So, facing the enemy, I picked up a supple, rubber-soled shoe from under a table and advanced towards the bed. A slight movement suggested the *grillo* was about to change position. I took a lightning swipe, it fell on to the pillow and then dropped out of sight, between pillow and bedhead. Inch by inch I moved my pillow away first, then the second one. There were two mattresses, leaving a tiny gap at the top corner as they lay side by side, down which the body (I hoped a dead one) had evidently slipped. Gingerly I tipped up my mattress and peered down—

no *grillo*. I lifted the corner of the other one—no *grillo*. Desperately I looked under the bed—no *grillo*. Little by little I unfolded the top sheet, my only covering. It wasn't there either. It must have fallen down into the springs somehow, and unless I was going to take the whole bed to pieces I had better give up. Which I did, thinking, hoping, that the *grillo* was well and truly killed. For the rest of the night I lay exhausted and fearful at the extreme edge of the bed, with the light on until the first pale fingers of dawn crept into the room through the narrow slats of the shutters. Then, wearily, I got to my feet to let in the morning. The air was cool and fresh; from a soft green on the horizon the sky paled to primrose. Gradually a rosy glow spread up and out to suffuse the land with the glory of a new day, and tinkle of bells announced an early shepherd on the move with his flock. But in my bed there was still a dead *grillo*, somewhere. I shuddered at the thought.

Punctually at the appointed time Nicolina arrived with breakfast, smiling a gay greeting. Did the *signora* sleep well? The *signora* shook a miserable head. 'There is another *grillo*, down there,' I pointed. Nicolina's eyes widened. '*Ancora, nel letto?*' 'Yes, in the bed,' I repeated bitterly. 'I hope you find it.' I hope they did.

*　　*　　*

Crickets notwithstanding we all parted the best of friends an hour later.

Beyond the long straight stretch that was Villanova Strisaili a sharp right turn led to a mountain road with so many acute bends that one lost count. At intervals tiny villages clung precariously to the green slopes above steep valleys, over them the mountains loomed, blue-shadowed as ever, a few peaks wrapped in wisps of softly moving cloud.

At Gairo women were at the communal water trough doing the household washing at a curve which now well-tried instinct made me take rather carefully. I found myself at the edge of a sheer drop, once more in the midst of a swarm of pigs, about fifty or sixty young ones this time, all squealing at the top of their

The Flumendosa Dam

The Poetto Beach, Cagliari, Sunday morning. Capo Sant'Elia in the distance

Playing the
launeddas, and
(*right*) At San
Pietro—making
a lobster basket

Conservation piece—
a *nuraghe* bronze in the
Cagliari museum

Alghero: the
harbour with
coral fishing
boats in
foreground

Alghero:
Catalan arches

voices. The wind had swept the din in the opposite direction so I had not heard them in advance. The lad in charge seemed quite unperturbed, however.

A signpost at an earlier crossroads had been anything but explicit, so I stopped to ask the way of an old man stumping up the hill. Over the other side of the valley lay what appeared to be a parallel road. What was far from clear from my present position was how, if at all, I reached it, and if I did, whether it was the right way to Cagliari. The old man gazed at me for a long, thoughtful moment. Yes, yonder was the road to the city, a much better one, he insisted, than the one I was on. He would have it I was now going in the wrong direction, which was true enough unless this road wound completely round. Did it? He didn't know. All he could say was that the opposite road went to Cagliari and this one was pointing the wrong way. Perhaps, he suggested, there was a better route back the way I had come. I gave up, and thanking him, accepted Hobson's choice. It was in any case impossible to turn at this point, so I continued, to find myself very soon at the head of a loop on a hidden bend, on the old man's 'better road'. I wondered if he had ever crossed to the hamlet opposite in his life.

Under the peaks, highly cultivated terraces of vines and small, green crops must have meant exacting labour, but like all *Sardo* husbandry I had seen, it was beautifully done, so clean, so neat.

Halfway down, towards an open plain the road narrowed to a single track at the entrance to a village, and in spite of road police, lights, signs and all possible paraphernalia, confusion was absolute, increased by the impatience of traffic that began to pile up in both directions, relatively little though it was in total. To angry hootings, perspiring road men, irritated police, and the steep angle of the road was added the menace of jay walkers, villagers on their lawful occasions but without a shred of understanding that sometimes it is a good thing to wait for a few moments. There were excited children, too, of course. Sard drivers, no less than other Italians, cannot bear to have another vehicle just in front or immediately behind, and resulting disputes—how I did wish I could understand *Sardo!*—reached a pitch that became almost hysterical. The only possible thing to do was to sit still until each of us could move in turn, but that was precisely what some just could not do. When the lights turned green they were in the road arguing with each other, or haranguing the world in general; when the colour changed to red they had just got back into their cars or lorries, ready to start. But even road blocks come to an end. Presently the way was clear and we were through the village. It was then I remembered the advice of a kindly driver when he handed a car over to me a few years previously: '*Signora, questa strada è molto pericoloso. Prego, piano, piano, e sempre a destra.*' So, on the best advice, I got well in to the right and let the world rush by.

On the big plain intense cultivation, much of it vines and other fruits, was broken by the bed of the river Cannas, nearly dry at this season, but as always, a paradise of flowers and oleanders whose scent drifted across the road, though there was little opportunity to look about here. On these level roads in the south cyclists, sometimes three abreast and all over the place, added to the more familiar hazards.

About twenty-five miles from Cagliari the route suddenly closes in, cut through sheer rock, green, looming, dark, completely serpentine, with ominous patches of retaining wall broken. At one stage I thought that notices: 'Car went over the verge here,' might have made a salutary dado. On the other hand, the cause of the damage could have been falls of rock regarding which there were several warning signs, suggestive of a grand opera type of finale to the accompaniment of full orchestra playing *fortissimo*.

It was beginning to rain, emphasising the sombre effect of being shut in by those enclosing heights, but the road surface was excellent, as nearly always with *Sardo* main highways.

At Quartu is a multiple crossroads. I stopped to ask one of the traffic police the whereabouts of the ESIT Poetto hotel, that by its name was obviously somewhere near the well-known beach. He pointed: 'Sharp right, then follow the sea, it is only a few minutes away.' This vast stretch of sand, just over six miles long, extends all the way from Quartu to the outskirts of Cagliari, the road running parallel with salt marshes on one side, the sea on the other. In the centre the big, new seven-storey hotel dominates the skyline, dwarfing all other buildings in sight. Built by *Ente Sardo Industrie Turistiche*, one of the two tourist organizations, it was opened in August 1964.

My fifth floor balcony gave a splendid view of the Gulf of Cagliari, right round from Capo Carbonara on the south-east, beyond the promontory of Sant'Elia in the middle, on to the Capo di Pula on the south-west, a distance of some twenty-eight miles. Beyond this lies Capo Spartivento, and still further, round a lovely bay, is Capo Teulada, the most southerly point of Sardinia, hardly more than a hundred miles from the coast of Tunisia.

*   *   *

With a population that has doubled since 1946 and now stands at about 200,000, the history of Cagliari, the capital of Sardinia, epitomises the confused and bitter history of the island as a whole. And though during the last World War it suffered severely from air raids, when nearly 50 per cent of the city was destroyed, there is still enough evidence of its ancient past to excite the interest of scholars and less knowledgeable travellers alike.

In the streets of Cagliari itself little is to be seen of the long Roman occupation other than the remains of the amphitheatre, its seats carved out of the living rock. But in the old quarter the many Pisan and Spanish influences are not difficult to identify. Some 500 feet above the port, from being a citadel built on a steep hill, basically designed to repel invasion, today the city has spread out along the waterfront. At the beginning of the fourteenth century it was on the heights, guarded by four immense Pisan towers set into the walls, towers stout enough to defy enemy cannon. Of these—the Eagle, the Lion, the Elephant, and San Pancrazio (generally known as the *Castello*)—only the *Torre dell' Elefante* and the *Castello* have survived. Of the original inhabitants and the original site of the city little is as yet certain.

147

According to an Italian encyclopaedia, Cagliari, then referred to as Caralis, or Kareles, was one of the earliest trading settlements established by the Phoenicians whose peaceful incursions, particularly in search of silver and other metals, were mostly limited to the southern coasts of Sardinia, and as well as Caralis, these included Nora, Sulcis, Bithia and Tharros. The encyclopaedia gives the relevant date as approximately the tenth century B.C., but Margaret Guido suggests at least two centuries later as probably being more correct.

Within a comparatively short period of the peaceful Phoenician invasion came Greeks; after them the warlike Carthaginians, against whom the indomitable *Sardi* revolted again and again; then followed the savage Roman occupation lasting some 700 years, Cagliari being established as a port for the Roman Fleet in 46 B.C. After the Romans there were the Vandals, once more, briefly, the Romans, then Byzantines and later, Saracens, who in A.D. 711 sacked and occupied Cagliari, forcing the luckless inhabitants to pay heavy ransoms including production from the silver mines.

Ninth century records speak of the *Giudici* for the first time, their number then unknown, and it was not until the beginning of the eleventh century that the four divisions of the island were established: that of Cagliari (for the south), Arborea (the centre), Logudoro (Torres), and Gallura (for the north-east), each with its governing *Giudice*.

By this time Pisa and Genoa, with encouragement from the then Pope, were struggling against each other for domination of the island, and against the Saracens entrenched in several areas. Eventually Pisan influence governed the south to a great extent, the Genoese holding the north, and by the end of the twelfth century the economy of all four *Giudici* had become subject to the authority of the two Italian cities. From the middle of the fourteenth century, however, the influence of the Vatican had shifted to the support of Alfonso IV of Aragon who, in 1356, besieged Cagliari and took it by force, defeating the Pisans. Some twenty years later Mariano IV, *Giudice* of Arborea, who had struggled ceaselessly against the foreign invaders, died of plague; his son was killed, and shortly after that his daughter, Eleanora, assumed authority in the name of her son, Federico, still a minor, she becoming *Giuditrice*, and a symbol to the whole island of resistance to invasion and tyranny. Tyndale compared her with Boadicea, suggesting that had she been ruler of a more important northern country she would have received wider and well deserved acclaim. She died about 1402, but not before, in addition to other activities, she had completed the work started by her father of codifying the Roman laws of Sardinia, never previously set down in proper form. So well was the work done that in 1421 her *Carta da Logu* was recognized by the Sard Parliament as valid for the whole island, and so remained for the next three centuries.

With the marriage of Ferdinand and Isabella in 1469, resulting in the union of Aragon with Castille, Sardinia was raised to the status of a Spanish dominion with a Viceroy whose headquarters were at Cagliari, a condition remaining in spite of sporadic opposition until 1714, at the time of the Treaty of Utrecht, when the island was ceded to the Elector of Bavaria. In exchange for Sicily, however, he handed it over to Vittorio Amadeo II, Duke of Savoy, who in 1720 was proclaimed first King of all Sardinia.

The eighteenth century as a whole was no less memorable than many others. During the wars of the Spanish Succession the English, allied to the Austrians, twice sent a fleet to the Bay of Cagliari, in 1701 and 1703 under Sir George Rooke and Sir Cloudesley Shovel. In 1708 another English sailor, Admiral Leake, in negotiation with the Spanish Viceroy, landed a small force and the city capitulated. But in 1713 the Spaniards were back—Philip V sent troops and ships to besiege Cagliari once more, and was successful. Much later, in 1793, it was the French who threatened, but a fortunate storm caused the invading fleet to withdraw, and on this occasion no harm appears to have been done.

In addition to foreign intervention, a century dating from 1720 was an unhappy one as far as native rulers were concerned, a period alternating between neglect and despotism, added to

Jesuit intrigues, which left the island in an even worse state than during the government of Spain, which had had its better moments. It was not, in fact, until the accession of Carlo Felice in 1821, and of his successor Carlo Alberto, that more liberal measures of justice and advancement were meted out to the unhappy Sards. Carlo Alberto's son, Vittorio Emanuele II, succeeding to the throne in 1861, finally united Sardinia with Italy, and the Spanish flag was gone from the *Castello* in Cagliari for the last time. Though not until 1948 was Sardinia at long last given a degree of autonomous government.

Even the *Sardo* coat of arms has suffered to some extent from the historical confusion of the island. There are still *Sardi*, as well as foreigners, who think that the cross with its quarterings of four black heads blindfolded with white bandages refer to four Moorish kings who, attempting to land at Cagliari, were defeated and subsequently beheaded for their pains. This apparently is no more than legend, the four heads set in the white cross of Savoy originally showing the white bandage round the forehead, and beneath a diadem, as a symbol of power. Why or when the bandages slipped, what has happened to the diadems, are questions no one appears to be able to answer, nor why the heads are black—though this could be due to Papal influence signifying victory over Islam. It is definitely asserted that the four heads have no connection with the *Giudicati*, even signifying government of the island as a united whole; certainly they each had their own individual coat of arms.

This, of necessity, is the barest skeleton of a history so involved, so desperate. But it suffices perhaps to demonstrate the tragic plight of a brave and intelligent people over many centuries whose rich territory happened to lie in the path of more powerful, ambitious nations; a people among whom, in the mountains, there always remained a core of those who would not submit to force, however much stronger, and whose successors' reactions to events of this day and age, with some reason, might be traced to generations of oppression, of loyalties, of resistance, and of blood.

*   *   *

From the ESIT Poetto hotel the route to Cagliari itself is quite straightforward, parallel with the sea and with the tramcars. At the entrance to the city it leads past the big football stadium, through the Piazza Amendola to the colonnaded via Roma. Here, among the shops and cafés, sitting at little tables under the sheltering arches at almost any hour of the day, can be seen a sample of the heterogeneous population of a whole area. Businessmen in town clothes sit discussing affairs, their juniors and lesser lights stop for refreshments or to buy cigarettes, girls giggle together, there are whole families come to do special shopping, tourists of several nationalities speaking their several languages, and threading through the crowd come long-skirted country-women, with purpose in their stride, sometimes with their men, in contrast to the short-skirted, high-heeled girls of the metropolis, and other urban ladies.

On the opposite side of the street, across the traffic, the clang of trams and whistles of the police, over the strip of green palms and magnolias, is the sea, with trading ships tied up alongside and those who serve them busy about their various cares. It gives an added, lively dimension to the scene that is wholly invigorating. Over all, immaculate, white-uniformed police held strict sway. But appealed to for advice in the matter either of parking or of direction I found them invariably helpful and courteous.

At the junction with the Piazza Matteotti, at right angles to the via Roma, the Largo Carlo Felice juts sharply uphill to the Piazza Yenne, and beyond it, leads to the narrow, one-way, high walled streets and alleyways winding in and out, up and down the old quarter. This is the citadel.

Set at the top of some steps the cathedral dominates a small square, and in its variety of styles typifies the history of the city. Originally built in the latter half of the thirteenth century in the late Romanesque pattern, it was remodelled in the seventeenth century and given a Baroque interior. Still later, in this present century, another façade was added in imitation of the earlier Pisan style. Inside are magnificent pulpits originally designed by Guglielmo for the twelfth-century cathedral at Pisa, and two great lions standing at the foot of the presbytery steps are by the same sculptor. There is the Baroque tomb of Martin II of Aragon, and in a tiny chapel the still more recent tomb of Marie-Louise of Savoy, wife of Louis XVIII of France. Outside, set into a wall at one side of the main door is a thirteenth-century stone carved with the arms of Pisa from which city it was originally brought.

Not far away the red wall of the University extends the whole length of a street. Founded in 1620 by Philip III of Spain, in its magnificent library of 150,000 volumes are many rare specimens, and an important collection of manuscripts includes *Giuditrice* Eleanora's original *Carta da Logu,* and the Dante Codex M 76. At the Institute of Physics within the University Antonio Pacinotti is said to have conceived and built the first dynamo.

Close by, the small, strikingly carved *Elefante* stands on its high ledge jutting from the powerful stone tower bearing its name, built in 1307.

In narrow alleys linking one small *piazza* to another faded shirts and other garments fluttering in the breeze proclaim the present occupiers of palaces once the homes of noble families. Handsomely proportioned windows and doorways with carved stone architraves, and walls sometimes bearing the arms of original owners, suggest past elegance. A steep passage along the old bastion wall just below the cathedral gives on to a large open square where children play, and from which one looks down on to the newer architecture of modern buildings, and across at the amazing thickness of the original wall.

Above this, leading off the Piazza Indipendenza is the pale, massive bulk of the *Torre di San Pancrazio,* the first of the four towers to be built, in 1305. From it is not only a tremendous view of the city, but also of the surrounding countryside and the bay. In this *piazza,* tucked into one side is the National Archeological Museum established in 1806 by Carlo Felice who gave his own private collection to start it going.

Though this museum has the excellent, if negative, merit of not being very large, it is nonetheless a storehouse of treasures, and I never did get to the first floor housing a picture gallery.

It was to the ground floor that I returned again and again to gaze at those small, attenuated bronze figures and other objects fashioned by the *nuraghi* people.

In the centre of the room enclosed in a world of their own by the protecting glass walls of their cases, their wit and their strength are quite outstanding, giving them a rare beauty and integrity. The largest is little more than a foot high, most are much smaller, some quite tiny, but these votive figures, animals, boats, carts (with spoked wheels) have a sureness of observation that is fascinating. They come from sites all over the island. From the temple at Serra Orrios is a cloaked warrior, erect and proud, broad-bladed sword borne on his shoulder, a large dagger carried across his chest; other warrior heroes have four arms and eyes, two shields and a pair of upstanding horns on their heads, presumably all indicating strength. Archers are particularly emphasised, one with a large feather on the end of a cane to show the force and direction of the wind—or so it is thought. From Ittiri is a man playing the *launeddas*, the triple pipes, one of the oldest existing types of musical instrument in the world today, still made and played in Sardinia. Animals include a wild boar, snout to the ground, obviously snorting and snuffling along. A trotting fox, nose up and forward, ears laid flat and brush extended in a straight line with the body conveys a truly life-like wariness, and perhaps fear. A small man sits astride a donkey, legs dangling comically just as one sees riders in the countryside today. A little bear shambles along—historically perhaps one of the most interesting bronzes in that bears as well as monkeys are thought to have preceded, not coincided with, human existence on the island. This tiny figure poses a question. A ceremonial boat with a stag's head forward of the prow and trellised gunwales has very much the rounded shape of sardine boats I saw later at San Pietro.

Three mother figures, seated, with a child, I was told represent a woman with a sick infant, a dead or dying one, and finally happy because the *bambino* has recovered. They do suggest just that.

Here are the neolithic Macomer Venus, one of the oldest exhibits, bones from the necropolis of the Domus de Janas, and one of the most amusing little models is in the form of a nuraghic type building at the side of which is a tiny square hut with a minute bird sitting on top, tail up.

At the entrance to the Punic Room is the *stele votiva* from Nora, a Phoenician tablet with signs representing the sun and moon below the script. Egyptian sphinx, Roman and Greek modelling in terracotta, and a wickedly humorous *Mamuthone* mask from Mamoiada—of a pig face—are in company with many differing exhibits including examples of obsidian glass with its lovely mother-of-pearl sheen. In the Roman Room headless statues of female figures have the familiar exquisitely carved drapery; a life sized Claudius Julius in full armour gazes down with empty eyes, and a hideous bust of Tiberius leers from its plinth, surely one of the most evil faces ever to be portrayed.

Different, but not least interesting, is the terrace at the top of the building where, among the flowers, exposed to sun and wind lie bits of stone carvings, pieces of lovely broken columns and capitals, statues and other treasures. Over the edge of the balcony in the sharp light one can look on the strength of those fortifications that even modern armaments failed to demolish, while across a section of the town and port, beyond an unbelievably blue sea the shape of Monte Teulada rises in the distance. To one side lie the salt marshes that, with others of the island, notably at San Pietro, represent important exports of salt to the *continente*. Tyndale, writing of them, also referred to the colonies of flamingoes that settled on these *stagni* from September to April. Describing their passage he said: 'These majestic and beautiful creatures . . . adopt in their flight . . . closeness to each other and steady simultaneous movement of their wings giving the appearance of one united mass. The exquisitely bright crimson of their plumage, slightly relieved by the paler hue of the inner feathers, resembles, when lighted by the sun's rays, a cloud of living fire . . . they appear at a moderate distance as a fringe of crimson silk lightly fanned by the passing breeze.' He quotes the *Sardo* name for them—*genterubie*—the crimson people.

At Nora, like a ghostly finger pointing back to the past, a single column stands at one corner of the Roman temple close to the edge of the sea.

Some twenty miles south of Cagliari, towards Capo Sparti-vento, the road to Nora passes first of all over a shallow neck of land, a shabby foreshore on one side, salt marshes on the other, across both of which gales blow with some force. It continues on between olive groves and orchards, past Sarroch dominated by oil refineries the flames from which flare dramatically at night, and are visible from a great distance, and finally through the little village of Pula, once described by Nelson as 'a delicious spot', to a small peninsula over a tranquil bay. At the far extremity it splits into two tongues of land, on the one a lone Spanish tower now used as a lighthouse guards the entrance to the water.

On the other side extensive and careful excavation during the last fifteen years, organized jointly by ESIT and the Superintendency of Antiquities, has resulted in a large area of the Roman town being uncovered. But the origins go back much further. Close to one group of Roman baths a Proto-Sard votive well has been found.

Legend as well as recent scientific investigation suggest that the founder was probably Norax, an Iberian chief from Tartessos, and the votive *stele* in the Cagliari museum, discovered as part of a monastery wall some miles away in 1774, originated in Nora when it was a busy Phoenician commercial colony. Later the Romans developed the town as an important seat of Imperial government linked to both Caralis and Sulcis. Here are not only baths, temples, a forum, theatres and wells, but also the sites of streets of shops, a foundry and other workplaces. At the edge of the shore still more remains of buildings are to be seen submerged under the clear water.

My first visit was the occasion of a party given one evening by ESIT for a group of French teachers of Italian. We all met at a little white chalet built by the tourist organization for such occasions near the ruins, and furnished with specimens of traditional Sard domestic craftsmanship which, as so often happens in such cases when untouched by modern 'improvements', is beautifully designed, beautifully executed, and wholly functional.

Here is the usual *cassapancha* of chestnut wood, expertly carved; wall hangings in vivid colours and various regional designs are round the room; on the floor carpets from Nule are tough and beautiful both in design and workmanship, larger ones each a month's work by a whole family. There are typical Campidano chairs of white wood, rush seated, comfortable, strong, the sides and backs painted in brilliant colours.

Outside, the company included a group of men and girls who give displays of Sardinian dancing and songs. Dressed in the elaborate Campidano costume, the girls wore pleated crimson velvet skirts bordered with rose and gold brocade, matching their aprons and slippers, with black velvet boleros over white cotton blouses, neck and cuffs frilled and embroidered. A short, gold-embroidered black ribbon hung over the head and down the cheeks of the girls, one of whom also wore the white lace wedding veil; '*la gitana*,' her friends called her. Certainly she had the dark, brooding look of that race. The men, in the basic black and white, trousers this time tucked into high black boots, also wore either dark red velvet or matching brocade waistcoats.

They were a cheerful company who danced and sang well, and, theirs the important role, the men were as light as cats on their feet, and as neat. The singing was best demonstrated towards the end of supper on the terrace when quite spontaneously, inspired by a suggestion from either a member of the troupe or a guest, they would start up. The men, in unison or in solos, sang in normal voice, but the girls, particularly *la gitana*, all had that strange, flat, wailing tone of the gipsy lament. But that was not all. Suddenly someone called 'Johnny Brown, Johnny Brown,' and forthwith Mario, with an accordion, sitting beside me, struck up *John Brown's Body*, though the last phrase was new to me—'*viva la libertà!*' It was sung with great relish in both *Sardo* and French, to be followed even more warmly by *Alouette*, again in both languages. Mario, a charming young man, to be married two months later and apt to fall off into a dream if the subject was mentioned, was a secretary in a boys' technical college. He was learning 'a leetle Anglish', had already visited Copenhagen and Berne, and had ideas of going to Barcelona for his honeymoon. Not London, I teased? He replied that he would like to come, but he thought that fog might not provide the happiest *ambiente* for a honeymoon. It is marvellous how the myth holds.

Opposite at the table were the tenor and the baritone of the party; the latter, the wag, with a lusty voice whose extemporising in the true Sard manner, if not always flattering to his companions, was highly diverting, and sung with a wicked rolling of eyes, to the accompaniment of much laughter among the others. Presently Mario, with a grin at me, started playing *Tipperary*, and this, too, was sung by everybody with tremendous gusto.

By this time the sun was almost gone, only a fading golden light shone on a pale sea so calm it looked like silk. The party repaired to the shore, and sitting on the rocks continued their own songs, in harmony, their voices hanging in the soft air to the accompaniment of one of their members playing the *launeddas*, the triple pipes, to whose music they had danced.

Of the three pipes, the longest and thickest, the *basso*, was about a yard long, attached to this was another about half the length and half the thickness—used for the accompaniment. The third, much the same size as the latter, and separate, with a very small, thin mouthpiece was the *canto*. The instrument was played with great skill by an elderly man, Antonio. The method is to use the cheeks as sacs for the air, breathing in through the nose and out through the mouth, which he did for an astonishing length of time without any distress. The obvious elasticity of his cheeks and neck was a marvel to behold. He said it took a long time to learn, he had started as a boy, made his own pipes, and search for the reed for the *canto* involved travelling some distance, I understood to the marshes of Oristano.

On the way back in the moonlight we passed the little church of Sant'Efisio, looking quiet now in the shadow of the night, but from May 1st to the 4th every year the centre of the greatest festival in Sardinia, the *Sagra di Sant'Efisio*. A General in the Roman army at the time of the Emperor Diocletian, Efisio was converted to Christianity and suffered death as a consequence. Later, threatened by plague in 1656, the Festival was instituted by the *Cagliaritani* in memory of his martyrdom in the hope of averting disaster, and ever since the anniversary has been celebrated with splendid pomp and great religious fervour.

On the morning of the first day the effigy of the saint in a magnificent gilded carriage flanked by police and mounted soldiers is taken in procession to the small church by the now peaceful bay, in the company of thousands of pilgrims on foot and on horseback, all clad in regional costumes. Following various religious services, at sunset on the fourth day a candle-light procession attends the return of the effigy to the city church in the Stampace district of Cagliari.

Meanwhile, horse racing and other displays, folk dancing and singing, and celebrations of all kinds mark the occasion which is considered as being the opening of the summer season.

* * *

The Poetto beach, like most playgrounds of the kind, has a rhythm of its own. And similar to the Platamona beach at Sassari is, in effect, in three parts. From the Cagliari side towards the centre is the Lido, complete with cabins, restaurant, cafés, music, dancing and all the more sophisticated facilities. In the centre is a stretch first with a limited number of private cabins, then of clear beach that includes a small section appropriated, though without obvious barriers, to the ESIT hotel. To this, early in the day, are taken chairs and umbrellas that add so much to the comfort of pleasant lazing. Beyond, towards the Quartu crossroads is an area for campers, extending across both sides of the road among pine trees, and well patronized.

During the week a limited number of holidaymakers and a few families with small children for whom this long, shallow stretch of sand is ideal, stake out their claims, but in the evening the whole beach is the playground of lithe young men, their statuesque bronzed bodies clad in the briefest of swimming trunks, alternately swimming, playing football, or just strolling back and forth. Girls, in groups, generally in miniscule bikinis, likewise wander up and down, this way and that, golden skins warm and glowing, eyes bright, hair blowing as they kick the white sands and pretend they aren't taking any notice at all of the attractive males. It is the Poetto version of the village Corso.

In the early morning of any day race horses can be seen being exercised along the shore, before the city is awake. But it is not until Sunday morning that the whole six-mile length of the Poetto becomes really thronged. Families begin to arrive soon after seven o'clock, children tumbling out of the family car, a slice of bread and something clutched in small hands, as they make for the lovely freedom of this pale, soft playground and shallow water bordering it. Parents and older folk disembark more slowly encumbered with umbrellas, chairs and other furniture. By ten o'clock not only is the whole Poetto crowded from end to end, but all the way to Capo Boi the route is lined with cars on both sides of the road, every small bay with its complement of regulars, tanned bodies lying stretched on towels or mattresses, or cutting through the transparent blue waters with practised skill. And from the shelter of Cagliari harbour a fleet of little sailing boats puts out from the special port reserved for them.

To my astonishment, however, by about 1.30 beaches and roads are comparatively empty once more, nearly everybody returns home for lunch, and until early evening peace reigns. But even then the parade is little more than on weekdays.

The road to Capo Boi, and beyond it to Villasimius is one of the most beautiful in the area. As I set out a light purple haze hung over sea and sky. A right turn at the Quartu crossroads led to a small bridge over a stream bordered with poplars their leaves shivering in the breeze, then on through tiny hamlets, each hardly more than a group of cottages—Mortorius, above a sparkling bay, Geremèas, with its red *cantonieri* house on a corner, and in the background, silhouetted against the mountains, a farmhouse ringed by orchards, olive groves and vineyards, every yard of ground carefully cultivated. A little stream ran down to the sea by villas tucked into niches, one, rosy-apricot in colour, built round an enclosed courtyard full of flowers visible from the road above. Still further uphill, the Taverna del Saraceno, originally a barn now owned and run as a *trattoria* by a Sicilian, marked steeply rising ground becoming sharper with each twist and turn of the road over promontories dropping sheer to the glittering water below, round the edge of bays of shining white sand.

On an open stretch without shade of any sort an unlucky man was wrestling with a punctured motorcycle. Under the blue sky in that blazing heat the glare was blinding. He shook an exasperated head at me and spread his hands with a typical shrug, poor thing. I gestured my sympathy, but there was nothing I could do to help.

On the left, all the time, the mountains rose higher and higher with the road. Typical *macchia*, patches of dried grasses, clumps of myrtle like big, dark green molehills broke the tawny blanket of cistus, now dangerously tinder dry and whose sharp, resinous tang was borne on the wind. Still higher and higher the road climbed, the sea, deep and far below, was almost hyacinth blue. Suddenly one was at the top, gazing down into a glorious blue bay, Capo Carbonara stretching away out into the sea, and beyond it the tiny island of Cavoli with its solitary watch tower. In the distance, down by the shore, just visible through a sheltering belt of pine and eucalyptus was the Grand Hotel Capo Boi.

Inevitably the garden of the hotel takes the visitor's eye first, spread out under the shelter of the mountain, reaching down to pale sand and limpid sea. Here, roses and violets, as well as more exotic arums and other lilies, bougainvillaea, oleanders, mimosa, bananas, and a hundred other flowering bushes and plants mingle in prodigal abundance. The tennis court, big swimming pool with special children's section, and the private beach all give promise of the excellence within.

Like most of the other first class *alberghi* in Sardinia, this hotel is recently built, just five years ago, to the design of an Italian architect, Matzetti. It is owned by a Swiss company, but the manager, Romano Romani, is an Italian from Sienna. The company has altogether 1,500 acres of surrounding land including mountains, enough to ensure privacy, sufficient also to necessitate careful guardianship in terms of fire, to which end there are permanent staff whose special duty it is to keep watch against this danger. Indeed, on my second visit ominous tongues of flame, seen dimly through a pall of thick smoke, were licking up the mountains in several places only a mile or so away.

*   *   *

Homer referred to the southern coast of Calabria, the Straits of Messina, particularly, as the 'violet coast', a title that could with justice also be given to the south of Sardinia. The sunsets of Cagliari are noted throughout the island, and that evening was one of the most marvellous spectacles of the kind I have ever seen, anywhere. The wind had dropped completely. From a rosy glow that embraced the whole arc of the sky the colour changed, very slowly, very gently, until sea, sky and land were together wrapped in a soft, luminous purple haze. Presently it brightened, with a momentary upsurging intensity of colour as though to reflect the wonder of the dying day, before it gradually deepened to a blue-grey ribbon lying so lightly on the sea and sand they almost seemed part of the sky.

Much later, about three in the morning, I woke. Opening the curtains I went out on to the balcony again. Straight ahead an enormous orange moon hung in the sky. Across the hardly moving water it shed a long shaft of golden light. The silence could be heard.

*   *   *

The most important nuraghic site in Sardinia is at Barumini, forty miles north of Cagliari. Not only is it one of the largest so far discovered in its total complex, but it is the first to be scientifically investigated, and the wealth of archaeological and other information it has yielded has thrown much light on the *nuraghi* people and their materials. According to Margaret Guido, chemical tests suggest the date of the original fort as being approximately 1270 B.C., that following Carthaginian raids in the sixth century it was razed to the ground, but rebuilt later, the clustering huts and other buildings around it being added to from time to time.

Most people who have seen others agree that this *nuraghe* is not the most interesting in terms of appearance, that Sant'Antine at Torralba is much more impressive, but this one, Su Nuraxi, is imposing enough, standing among the corn lands within a fringe of lesser *nuraghi* on the horizon, and with a desolate, ruined castle on the extreme tip of a sudden steep cone of land jutting up at Lasplassas in the near distance.

Barumini lies on the northern edge of the Campidano, a long tract of low, rolling, fertile land extending diagonally for some sixty miles from Cagliari to beyond Oristano on the west coast. For more than 2,000 years this area has provided an abundant supply of excellent quality corn, not only for the island itself, but also for the *continente*. It was the granary of Imperial Rome for centuries.

From Cagliari the route follows the main *autostrada* to the north through Monastir and Serrenti, but a confusing triangle of crossroads at Villasanta, Sanluri and Furtei proved a hazard as I had left my road map behind. Strange as it may sound in view of the importance of the *nuraghe*, there was not one signpost carrying the name of the village until I actually reached Barumini itself.

The sun blazed out of a cloudless sky and several times on the way there were little groups of men and women selling fruit by the roadside, big luscious melons piled high, peaches, apricots and grapes all laid out appetizingly, while the families themselves sheltered from the sun under large black umbrellas held close over their heads. On my return in late afternoon I observed there had been plenty of takers, supplies were well down. I had pulled up at one stall in the morning to ask if there were any figs. They had none, then, but a woman promised some if I would care to stop on my return. When I arrived there she was, not only with figs, but with figs most elegantly packed in a little container made of the dark, scented leaves bound with plaited straw. The whole family clustered round, apparently delighted to have a customer so pleased with their efforts.

Further on, just beyond Furtei, sugar beet pickers of both sexes and varying ages were having a mid-morning break, also sheltering under black umbrellas on the ground. They were a gay and friendly bunch.

From now on patches of vines enclosed within prickly pear hedges broke the burnt gold of corn stubble on the outskirts of Barumini, the village itself consisting of a few colour-washed cottages, and others behind that anonymous mask of high walls and big wooden gates. But tell-tale climbing roses hung over some of the barriers, the tops of oleander bushes were visible wreathed with bougainvillaea, and hollyhocks nodded here and there, speaking of a gentler attitude than might otherwise have seemed apparent. At a crossroads I pulled up to ask the way and went over to speak to a small, grey-haired woman who had appeared at the entrance to her gateway. She gave me directions, then added that it was a very hot day, would I care to rest a little, or perhaps have a drink of water.

Maria Gaddoni's little courtyard garden was as neat and clean as a new pin, the surrounding walls and those of the house at ground level all whitewashed. Among the cobbles that paved the yard, beautifully and evenly set, feathery, bright green plants each about a foot high looked fresh and cheerful, others bore yellow flowers, roses climbed a wall, two placid, well fed cats blinked sleepily in the shade, and a youth sat under the shelter of a young acacia tree. Steps at one side led up to the house, chairs and a table under the balcony with arum lilies in pots made a pleasant spot from which the small owner could take the air. When I left she bade me to be sure to stop on my way back if I had need of another drink of water, or a rest.

The *nuraghe* stands behind a protective hedge bordering the road, a bulky-looking ruin with scant, dry grass growing untidily all over it in between the blocks of stone of the outer wall, and covering the tightly packed footings that are all that remain of buildings that once closely surrounded it. Margaret Guido offers a fascinating diagram of the original fortification as it is imagined to have been. But even now, inside, interest quickens. In the heart of the fortress a huge tower, still three storeys and some fifty feet high—thought originally to have been even higher —is surrounded by a very narrow corridor, with steep and confusing steps, dim and precipitous anyhow in terms of movement within, to an enemy seeking forcible entry, an obvious death trap. It was not difficult to imagine the desperate and dreadful struggle that must have been necessary to capture such a place. Four smaller towers, equally difficult of access, are still there, and a well; and lower than ground level what I was told must have been the grain and other stores, certainly here designed with an understanding of draughts, for the air was not only cold, it was also very fresh. Niches for sleeping, in which some years ago two skeletons were discovered—among the few so far found—gave clues to the size of the occupants, one having been about five feet tall, the other very slightly more. Why did they die alone like this, and how? The question thrust itself forward instinctively.

From the highest point of the tower as it can be climbed today the commanding view of the countryside is immense, originally it must have enabled good warning to be given of encroaching enemies, and perhaps signals to the outlying, lesser *nuraghi*. Now a criss-cross pattern of cornfields marches away into the far distance broken only by the village on a hummock of land, and that strange castle at Lasplassas.

My guide, a small, harassed young man, who appeared from nowhere as I was wandering alone among the stones, took a poor view of a woman by herself, and I had some sympathy for him. It was very hot, and from a vantage point half-way up the inner tower I had seen three people moving off in a car I had not previously noticed. The guide had evidently been climbing up and down, in and out with them, and on such a day the energy needed for the exercise was considerable. To do it all over again, and to remember the patter he had evidently been taught, was almost too much on this torrid noon. Midday pressed on him with all its demands. So eventually I offered to give him a lift back to the village, which he refused, saying it was too hot, and taking off his jersey started to walk the long mile down the blistering road, muttering.

*   *   *

Time was running out. Next morning I left Cagliari on the last leg of my journeying in the south—now to visit the island of San Pietro, which legend has it was named after the saint who was shipwrecked there in a storm. As I was to stay a final few days at Santa Margherita on my return I took the northern road, via Iglesias, the rich mining centre, to Portoscuso, from which the ferry runs to the island.

Through the Cagliari suburbs, passing the airport at Elmas, the route was quite straightforward, taking a left fork at Decimomannu, named from the Roman milestone found there with an inscription stating that this marked the tenth mile to Sulcis from the capital. By this time city houses were beginning to be left behind, the *autostrada* leading along the southernmost edge of the Campidano through open country, past miles of corn stubble broken by small vineyards enclosed in their prickly pear hedges, then, after Siliqua, through an area of dry grasses dotted with small, shrunken, wild pear trees and cork oaks known as the *Prato Africano*. On the right was Domusnova with its immensely long caves, on the left two lone peaks raised solitary heads above the plain, one, the Monte del Sulcis, the other, topped by the ruined thirteenth-century Castello del'Aqua Fredda, built during the fight against the Spaniards, and now as bleak and forlorn as the one at Lasplassas on the way to Barumini.

A feature of this road were the old houses of *lardus*, a special brick of straw and earth, an ancient and excellent fabric for keeping out heat in summer and cold in winter. The same material is much used for wine storage which, throughout Sardinia, is always at ground level, never below. Houses of this fabric were generally built in the Arab style, with the enclosed inner courtyard built inside the open square of the home; some of the older houses in country and especially in mountainous regions being said also to have rooms rounded at the corners so that evil spirits could not hide there, and so do mischief to the household. And on this Iglesiante road the *Sardo* liking for brilliant colours held full sway, sometimes with two shades together such as bright pink and yellow, parrot green with yellow, lilac and pink.

With Carbonia, due south, Iglesias—the name a derivation from the Spanish *Villa della Chiesa*—forms part of what has been the most important Sardinian mining centre from earliest times. Here came Phoenicians, after them warlike invaders one following another, seeking the mineral wealth to be found in plenty. Here, too, is mainland Italy's only supply of coal, not of a very good quality; and more important in total, probably, is the iron, zinc, the lead, and other metals, at one time even more precious ones, especially silver. And here, as I passed through the busy, flower-lined streets of Iglesias to the outskirts, were once more the countrywomen, often with big, round baskets on their heads, and that shy, revealing smile in response to a greeting on the road.

The earth had changed colour, as the winding road, cut through the hillside, revealed all sorts of tones from the pale, sandy gold to chocolate, tawny red-browns, and a deep bluish tint. A group of abandoned miners' cottages gave a momentarily desolate air, but a little further on were the new dwellings, once more in a rash of violent colours. The sound of heavy machinery was borne on the wind with the scent of mimosa from gardens, and as the road turned still further, hills became lower, rounder, there was a scent of figs, and of the sea. Then one was climbing again, looking down and across at Iglesias in a green valley, from where I presently stood, the road still rising, the tang of the sea even stronger. White clouds scudded across the sky. At the side of a sharp hill a horse and cart were drawn up, beside them a very small man with a stubble of grey beard and the quick, challenging eyes of a bird. More than thirty years a miner, he said he now had 'a very small pension, but something'. The beautifully tilled land immediately in front of us, and a small vineyard were his. 'Yes, it's lovely, but you can't eat it.' He was nearing seventy and finding the work heavy. His sons were both married, and they had families now, in any case one lived in Cagliari. He shrugged, then suddenly brightened at the thought: 'I am a grandfather of four boys. Four boys.' The emphasis showed his pride. Here at least was the promise of continued ownership of land so hardly won.

The road swept up a little further to spread out on all sides, covered with low scrub, mostly myrtle in bloom. At the edge mine shafts reared their ugly bulk, cables carried the buckets continuously across the skyline, and at the coast four smoking chimneys and a long buttress of rubble signified electricity works. A straggle of houses indicated Portoscuso and I asked the way to the jetty of the only individual in sight, who appeared to be the village simpleton. He assured me the way lay down there, and sent me miles past the correct turning, but realizing I had gone too far I came back, to seek my usual source of help. The man at the petrol pump was sympathetic. '*Cretino*,' was his comment on my previous informant. 'I will tell you the way, *signora*. Trust me and you won't go wrong. The road is by that black car and the square tower. Turn right down there, it is a *strada bianca*, but a good one, and it will take you to the port in five minutes.' He was right about the direction and the time needed, so I had to forgive him the 'good *strada bianca*,' which turned out to be a badly potholed dirt track.

The boat would not leave for another hour, so I went to the hotel for lunch. Everything at the Albergo Panorama was spotlessly clean, the cloakroom even boasted of fresh hand towels, plural. I lunched on grilled mullet, freshly caught, and the only quarrel I might have had was the price of these delicious fish—almost ten shillings for two medium sized ones—though I knew they were not so common, or so easy a catch. But I enjoyed my meal on a terrace over the bright water looking across at San Pietro and San'Antioco, and nearer at hand watching a domestic drama of some small children scuttling hither and thither in shallow water like little fishes trying to evade the net. Eventually their elderly nurse, grandmother, or whatever she was, just waded in and brought out two by the scruff of the neck amid loud squeals; but victory was conceded, the rest of the brood, accepting defeat, followed meekly.

After the fish and some cheese, what would I like demanded the waiter. I said some fruit please, if possible a peach, a ripe one. Which, strangely enough, is not always appreciated any more than is a ripe tomato. They are preferred firm and unripe. The waiter reappeared with a basket of delicious apricots, peaches and grapes. With care he chose a splendid peach, which he laid on the plate in front of me with a pleased smile. '*Ecco, signora, è bellissima.*' It was, too.

Down at the port, the *Arbatax*, spruce and white, another Tirrenia ferry, this time from Genoa, was taking in oil. Passengers-to-be must wait. So I strolled down the quay. Sea-gulls were wheeling on the ebb and flow of the wind, and another, largish sea bird with long legs and a strong curved beak that a couple of long-distance lorry drivers insisted was a stork, and was not. A dredger was at work in the central channel, 'always,' I was told, and a dock wall extension designed to enable more and heavier traffic to be accommodated added to the usual clutter of a wharf. In addition there was a long gantry for loading metal ore. In the distance Monte Teulada was visible far on the skyline. Overhead, clouds had begun to gather.

Eventually we were all aboard and away, not without potential drama. As the ship turned in the harbour a small boat with one white and one yellow sail appeared to be about to cross straight in front of the bows of the oncoming *Arbatax*. Screams of alarm from passengers were met with gay nonchalance from the helmsman, however. 'Oh, the fishes don't get enough to eat here, anyway.' In fact both craft were on the point of turning away from each other as he well knew, but there were sighs of relief all round when the manoeuvre became apparent.

Out in the channel the ship began to roll in a quite heavy swell and silence fell on deck. But the water was still so clear that white sand, rocks and seaweed were each distinct on the sea bed down below all the way. By the time we docked, about twenty minutes later, rain was coming down well and truly. Where was I going, demanded a young sailor as he unhooked the holding rope from the car. To the Hotel Riviera I replied. He grunted disapprovingly. 'Well, you'll sleep well enough, but you won't eat well there.'

At the reception desk of the hotel they were expecting me. A single room had been reserved, but only double rooms had bath or shower. I enquired how much this would cost and during the conversation an elderly chambermaid appeared at my side, to join in the discussion. 'But,' she objected, 'that room has a double bed, and sheets for two,' looking at me severely. 'I have made it for two,' she insisted, 'they are big sheets.' Her glance suggested that a lone woman demanding a *letto matrimonio* was up to no good, bathroom or no bathroom. The young man at the desk tried to placate her. 'The *signora* is paying for it.' But the chambermaid was not having any truck with this sort of wickedness. She snorted and disappeared. I only saw her afterwards when she brought my breakfast each morning with tight lips and a quick, furtive look round the room. I felt she would have liked to have looked in the wardrobe or under the bed.

The chambermaid's protests notwithstanding, my baggage was duly carried to the room with the *letto matrimonio*, and having unpacked and washed my hands in the trickle of water which was all that came out of both hot and cold taps, I went down to an excellent lunch of lobster caught overnight and cooked that morning. It was tender and delicious, and remembering the comments of the sailor on the ferry I decided that his criticism must have had some personal element in it. Unhappily, he proved to be right, this being the only good meal I had there. I may have been unlucky, enthusiastic friends who stayed there briefly only a few days earlier were contented; but it is also significant that several times in Carloforte, villagers who enquired where I was staying demanded to know how I found the food at the *albergo*.

Whether the saint did or did not land on San Pietro it is well named. A small, rocky island, the greater part of its coast rises almost sheer out of the sea, its sparse soil barely covering the grey, volcanic rock, the red porphyry and obsidian, offering little generosity for cultivation. Roughly in the shape of a triangle, it is seven miles long on the eastern side, the base, and five miles across to the apex on the west, Carloforte in the centre of the east coast being the only settlement. Though evidence of habitation goes back a long way, beyond the Punic era, and traces of still more ancient pagan cults have been found, the present colony dates from 1737 when the Genoese island of Tabera off the north coast of Africa was overrun by Tunisians. Carlo Emanuele III, King of Sardinia, gave permission for the luckless Italians to be settled on San Pietro, but even then their troubles were not yet over. In 1792 they were invaded by the French and eventually rescued by the Spanish, though not before they had burned their newly developing village in a desperate attempt to obstruct the enemy.

And high above the port today the ruins of a long wall bear witness to defence against the Saracens. Which helps to explain why Nelson, when he called with his fleet in 1798, was not at all hospitably received, an event to which he was not accustomed in Sardinia, and which he recorded with some asperity.

As a result of this unhappy history there is not a little wry humour on the subject of communication with the adjacent island—so-called—of San'Antioco. The people of San Pietro speak *Genovese*, those of the latter island *Sardo*, so modern Italian has to be used as a common language.

By late afternoon the rain had stopped, a timid sun appearing in a pale sky as I set out to explore. The waterfront stretches the whole length of the village. Opposite the hotel small motor boats and similar craft were corralled; in the centre, dominated by a large statue of Carlo Emanuele III, lies the main quay with ticket and harbour offices, and either side of which the ferries and cargo ships are docked. Further down, hedged by a wall of their own, the fishing boats are anchored. One or two large early nineteenth-century buildings with elegant balconies make an imposing background to the *piazza* with its trees and little tables; behind, the village rises steeply, with countless stone steps at every twist and turn. As I climbed, panting, to yet another level, a group of women sitting together, sewing, watched me. 'Have you counted them?' called one. 'No, have you?' I replied, at which there was general laughter.

Down at the fishermen's wharf men were mending nets, dyed blue because they are then said to be invisible to the fish. The men bless the nylon because it is stronger than the old line, and the now common plastic floats that replace the traditional cork. 'But there is still mending, mending, mending, every time we go out,' complained one wearily, holding up his handiwork for inspection.

In a shed among the usual clutter of baskets, nets, floats, oars and other tackle, a boat was being built, to me a never-ending source of fascination, watching the skill and confidence with which the men construct so small and comparatively frail a defence against the tremendous might of wind and wave. Mediterranean storms are sudden and violent. At the end of the harbour neglected buildings marked all that is left of a former cannery.

At one time, also, mining on San Pietro was a profitable industry, but now, abandoned workings and ruined cottages are all that remain of that occupation. Fishing is today the main support of the inhabitants, tunny fishing in the brief season their especial interest. It calls for two qualities they have in abundance: skill and strength, and offers two other things they need: money and excitement. I asked if the *mattanza* had been a good one this year. It had. The great fish, many heavy with eggs, had swarmed into the island nets, into the *camera della morte*. Shoals had not gone north at all this time, as I had already learned at Stintino.

In contrast to the highly organized and profitable tunny fishing was the activity of a small boat in the harbour. Roping one end of a net into a ring on the wall, the fisherman then rowed in a wide circle, the net being dropped steadily overboard until the wall was again reached, this time at the top end of the harbour, by open water. Then, inside the ring, a huge stone tied with rope was dropped into the sea with a resounding thump, to be heaved out again, the performance being repeated every few yards. This continued for about twenty minutes before the net was gradually drawn in, a few silver flashes churning the water on the final haul. After which the whole laborious business began all over again. It seemed a tedious way to frighten fish into a net, but I was assured it was 'a very old custom indeed. No one knows how old.'

A couple of sardine boats, painted bright green and white, were being got ready for the night's work. Larger than other fishing craft, they had prow and stern curving high out of the water, a perilous-looking superstructure over the bows holding several rows of shallow wooden boxes for the catch. The shape was much as I had seen in *nuraghi* bronzes in the Cagliari museum.

Another, different, boat preparing to set forth, had an astonishing Emmett-like funnel rising from the engine, belching smoke and fumes. Andrea, the fisherman in charge, had with him two young sons. They were going 'far out', would I like to come? 'You go, *signora*,' urged a couple of mates on the quayside. 'You'll be all right, he's a clever sailor.' I didn't doubt it, but there was no time to go back for a thick sweater. I was clad only in a thin cotton shirt and trousers and knew that '*fuori*' it would be very cold through the night, so, regretfully, I thanked him but refused the invitation, and wishing him good luck turned to climb still more steps.

At the top of the village, behind the fisherman's quay, was a desolate piece of rocky, waste land flanked by a row of tiny houses. Each had a minute garden full of flowers, each was as neat and clean as the next. And sitting in his porch was a man weaving the big lobster baskets. I had asked to see this, looking for such a man whenever I had been at the coast, anywhere, without success. Now here he was. Beside him lay two tidily bound piles, one of long thin canes, the other of shorter, dark, straight sprigs of myrtle each bearing its little tuft of fresh green leaves on the end, demonstrating the newness and suppleness of the twigs to be plaited horizontally round the long canes. The light was going, so I asked if I might come on the morrow to take a photograph. Of course, they said, the wife adding that her husband would start a new basket for me in the morning as this one was nearly finished.

There is no highway encompassing the whole island of San Pietro, and only two roads, leading in opposite directions from the port, can be described as reasonably good. One, going due north, leads to the Punta Tonnara and the canning factory, as might be expected, past what is obviously the more prosperous section of Carloforte with larger villas behind garden fences, and with a wide view across the port to the mainland.

I headed in this direction directly after breakfast next morning. It was another glorious day, though a stiff breeze still blew. Down at the point a strong sea was running, pounding the vivid water onto the rocks with a roar that almost drowned the voices of gulls swaying on the wind, throwing foam high into the air like a white wall to fall on the short turf or into pools. Further out, in deep water, the sea was sapphire blue. Behind a stout fence the tunny canning factory and offices were shuttered and deserted. On a small hill at the edge of the sea a builder trying to roof a cottage was having trouble with the wind.

Back at the quay were my friends of yesterday, including Andrea and the net menders. To enquiries as to the success of the night's fishing all shook lugubrious heads. 'The weather is never good for fishermen when Portoscuso is so clear,' said one, ruefully. Andrea had had little more than five kilos, one of the sardine boats had not yet returned, the second had not had much of a catch.

Up the hill Silvio Sensis of the lobster baskets was working on a new one as promised. Yesterday's basket was finished. Most of the island girls and women were good looking, but Silvio Sensis' wife must have been a raving beauty in her youth. Now, white haired, with grown children and years of toil behind her, the worn face was still lovely, spoilt only by those missing teeth; but neither time nor a hard life had marred the beautiful bone structure of her face, the lively expression of the large hazel eyes. She had a gift for me, a big conch shell, a splendid one, even if it did stink to high heaven. They are not very common and this, a female about four years old, I was told, was a special one.

From next door came a very pregnant daughter with some tiny, but equally beautiful shells, and a couple of neighbours each proferred one. I could only thank them, almost with a lump in my throat. They had so little, but they shared that with a stranger, and gaily. I thought that if I had offered to buy the shells they would have been deeply offended. I hope I was right. Other *Sardi* friends later confirmed that I was.

Then one woman had an idea. At the Porte Leone, she reminded the others, they were tying sardine hooks. The *signora* should see that too. So they led me round to La Cinta, another piece of waste land, this time sheltered by the remains of a high stone wall, all that was left of the once stout defence against the Saracens, giving a sweeping view of the coast, with arrow slits in the walls, and a gateway, the Porte Leone. In the shelter of the wall sat a little group tying small hooks to fine lines, then sticking each as it was finished on to the edge of a plastic basin banded with cork. Into the basin went the lines, dropped apparently carelessly, but with an accustomed skill so that any hook could be lifted out without entangling the whole. Children flocked around, and a woman smilingly demanded to know whether I would like to buy a *bambino* as a souvenir. There was general laughter, but it had an unhappy undertone. As I had already learned, when the mines had been working, as well as the little cannery, there had been enough for all. Now there was only fishing, which meant too many men chasing too few fish and an insufficient market, with so much depending each spring on the all important and uncertain *mattanza*.

Questions followed, quick and searching. Where had I been? What did I like most of what I had seen? when had I come? how long would I be staying? I said that I had arrived yesterday and was sorry to be leaving the next day. At which point I turned to go to the shelter of the *Porta* in order to change a film. An elderly man hurried after me. Would I perhaps prefer to come to his home to do this? It was only opposite. We returned shortly to the group, to what had obviously been a discussion about me. One man looked up with an engaging, challenging grin. I had not had nearly enough time to see San Pietro properly, and in any case it was difficult for a stranger to know where the paths led. His name, he said, was Giovanni Mereu; if he came to my hotel at two o'clock this afternoon would I like to make a tour of that part of the island I had not seen, with him as guide? There were not many roads but he knew them all. He hoped I wouldn't mind using my car, but he hadn't one. I said, yes please, to general murmurs of approval.

Punctually at the appointed hour Giovanni Mereu arrived. In his mid-thirties, I thought, with an intelligent face, brown hair, honest brown eyes, and the fine, tanned, but not dark complexion I had already noticed among the other fishermen. Short and stocky he gave the impression of immense physical strength, and of endurance. He hesitated as we were getting into the car. '*Signora*, these are not good roads, like the via Tonnara. There is a *brutta strada*.' I replied that we would go as far as possible, anyway, which seemed to please him.

How right he was soon became evident. *Brutta strada* was a mild description, as we bumped and slithered gingerly along the tracks, all four wheels rarely on the same level among the treeless scrub. First we drove south, climbing until we could go no further, then continuing on foot to one of the highest parts of the island. All round was the low *macchia* of dry cistus and blackberry clipped by gales; at the edge of the cliffs, nearly a thousand feet below us, blue sea foamed over red porphyry rocks, snaking into the wide semicircle of Medzaluna Bay, sliding up over white sands. The cries of sea birds were borne up faintly on the wind as they soared and dipped endlessly, white specks against the dark rocks, and still darker entrances to grottoes plainly visible. Above, cottonwool clouds were racing across the blue sky. Straight ahead, some hundred miles of blue-green water lay between us and the northern coasts of Africa whence had come invaders all those centuries ago.

Now we took a westerly tack, down and down, over an even worse road. At one moment Giovanni Mereu looked at me doubtfully. How much more of this would I take, his look said. But so far, so good, at a snail's pace, but no matter. He led us down to La Caletta, past a small children's camp set among

sheltering eucalyptus and pines, housing cheerful, noisy youngsters, and still further down to a strange, narrow-necked stony
bay, past old lead workings and zinc mines surrounded by tiny
forlorn, ruined houses, to a rocky beach protected on one side
by steep cliffs of pale limestone blocks that looked as if someone
had just piled lump on lump in some mad, giant's game. On the
opposite point, protecting the quiet water, rose cliffs equally
high, but as dark, almost as black, as the opposite ones were
light. It was an extraordinary juxtaposition in this lonely, de-
serted place.

As we clambered over the rocks my guide shed his shoes,
wandering in and out of the water, finding sea urchins, showing
me how to judge which were the edible female ones, which the
males with nothing to eat inside. We also found some pretty
shells, and at one moment he came up with a young squid, its
revolting, slimy grey tentacles dangling from his hand. His face
fell when I drew back—'I thought it would please you.'

Presently we turned, to follow a narrow, broken road to the
lighthouse, on the extreme western point of the island, the apex
of the triangle, passing in sheltered valleys some small vineyards.
Each family has its own plot, and in September nearly the
whole of Carloforte, bringing goods and chattels necessary for
their stay, repairs to these vineyards for the grape harvest,
families helping each other. In total, did they make out, I asked?
'We eat, but no more,' was the reply.

Giovanni Mereu was one of a number of islanders who had
ranged further afield. As a *marinero* he had been to South
America and to European ports in Scandinavia and Germany,
but never to Britain. Best of all he preferred the *mattanza*, only
wishing it lasted longer.

At the lighthouse the wind shrieked like a banshee round the
sturdy stone tower, through radio wires, and tore at family
washing flapping wildly though it was in a comparatively sheltered corner. A small garden was making a brave effort to
justify the work involved in the shallow earth. We were higher
than over the Cala Medzaluna, though it was quite hot, and
as we gazed out over this tremendous vista of sea and sky facing

due west across the Mediterranean, leaning on the wind, rocking a little on our feet, far away a ship came into sight. Only a speck in the vastness, yet it instantly closed the circuit, giving human point to this lofty isolation. In an office the radio began to chatter.

On the way back we made a detour to pass alongside the marshes and a salt lake, big heaps of the greyish-white powder spread to dry out, prior to export to the mainland and some to the *continente*.

Giovanni Mereu had some shells he wanted to give me as a souvenir and suggested he should bring them to my hotel at eight o'clock. Dead on time he arrived. From the reception desk they telephoned to say *un signore* was asking for me, but before I could so much as get to the door of my room there was a knock. Outside stood my host of the afternoon, all spruced up, faded shorts and old cotton vest changed in favour of spotless trousers and white shirt. By his side stood a small girl, his daughter of whom he had told me. An only child—he had regretted with the usual shake of the head, reminding me of Luigi in Sassari. This was *brutta figura* again.

Little Maria Mereu was eleven, dark haired, dark eyed, with a sweet, candid young face. Dressed in her best, a pretty yellow cotton frock, she shyly proferred a small packet. It contained two baby crabs of a special kind (very dead), as specimens, and some shells. She hoped I would like them. Her father apologized for the fact that his wife had not come as she was not well. I suggested we all go down to the bar and perhaps Maria would like a Coca-Cola or other drink. She flashed an appealing look. What, I asked, was it that she would specially like? Again there was that appealing glance, this time directed at Giovanni Mereu; he smiled back at her and replied that most of all she would like a ride in my car, she had never been in one. So we piled in, Maria in front with me. She would like to go to the Punta Tonnara, and would she like to go fast or slowly? 'Fast, please,' in a shy whisper. But father said, no, slowly please. So we split the difference, the child's eyes bright with excitement, though she sat quiet and tense. Presently we returned to the hotel and repaired to the bar. Now, her choice was a chocolate ice cream, which in due course she finished with an enormous sigh of contentment. 'Another?' But she shook her head. 'No thank you.'

Next morning I took the ferry to Calasetta on San'Antioco, for one reason only not sorry to leave. The trickle of water in which I had washed my hands on arrival had been the first and last in that bathroom. And even lavish use of witch hazel doesn't compensate for good, plain water, hot or cold.

San'Antioco is the site of the original Sulcis, some of which can still be seen submerged beneath the clear blue water by the shore. It is always referred to as an island, and is so called on maps. In fact it is connected to the mainland by a narrow causeway. From Calasetta on the north-eastern tip of the island to the little town of San'Antioco itself is some twelve miles, mostly through inhospitable land where, in the shallow soil, hardly-won stretches of vineyards or other crops break the rugged outline of stony outcrop or sandy turf. The town proved larger and busier than I had anticipated, splendid oleanders lining the streets and scenting the air, and there were quite a lot of people about. Rugs and traditional wall hangings, *arazze*, are made here, and searching for the *Pro-loco*, I passed workrooms with women and girls weaving them. But again I was defeated by that wretched luncheon closure; the offices were shut and locked, no one in an adjoining building could offer any useful suggestion, so off I went. It was then only noon and I could not wait some three or four hours.

Over the narrow neck of land the smell of fish and salt marshes once more assailed the nostrils, but a few miles further on began a beautiful stretch of road bordered all along one side with tall eucalyptus trees. At a sharp right turn a pretty girl was busy with the family washing at a trough under a clump of poplars, and from there the route towards Porto Botte led past farmlands, olive groves and orchards, one or two lovely, apricot-tinted houses roofed with rose-red or greenish-brown tiles blending perfectly with the tones all round. Still on an excellent *autostrada*, another sharp turn, this time to the left, led to Giba, with Monte

Teulada clear in the distance, tawny cistus brown, matching the copper-coloured earth, an '*Africano*' landscape again, while at the immediate roadside bamboos, tamarisks and figs offered cool, scented greenness.

It was another of those golden days, the sky dotted with occasional small white clouds moving lazily in the heat of noon now pressing down, the sun so directly overhead that the shadow of the car lay exactly underneath the vehicle. Shutters and doors of houses were all closed, presenting the blank and empty face to which I was now accustomed, and leaving me the only being abroad.

Teulada, partly Moorish, partly Spanish in origin, lay sweltering in its valley at the foot of the mountain, and I decided to stop here for lunch, at the Albergo Sebera, which didn't on the face of it look very inviting. Outside, and most unexpected for Sardinia, was a litter of dirt and rubbish, in the midst of which on an ordinary upright chair lolled a big man in his shirtsleeves. Not a very clean shirt either. None of which boded well for the interior. It proved, however, to be better than might have been expected, and though simple, adequate. A party of French tourists, two families, had already spread themselves down a long table with the usual amount of noise, added to by one small daughter of about three, an enchanting looking child with long, blonde curls and angel face, whose idea of lightening the tedium of grown-up eating was alternatively banging a door shut, or, when that palled, thumping an adjoining table with a large spoon. Her elders took no notice, just getting on with their eating and chatting, the child, remembering food from time to time, wandering to her mother's side mouth wide open for a spoonful, for all the world like a hungry bird. After a while she decided it was altogether too hot and started doing a strip-tease, when she was taken sharply in hand, to the tune of piercing screams, overturned glasses and a broken plate.

The party, the other side of the room from me, had no idea of my nationality, and did not themselves speak Italian, except for the odd word, getting what they wanted mostly by signs. One of the men, to indicate that he required two portions of ice cream held up his hand in the famous V sign, adding '*due Churchill*,' which our waiter, a small, most competent lad who told me proudly that he was twelve, understood at once, amid much laughter.

The roast veal and a salad of tomatoes was good, but there was neither *Sardo* nor mainland Italian cheese, only *Gruyère*, which didn't please the French guests either. And the only fruit consisted of very unripe apricots or peaches.

From Teulada the winding, switchback road led up and up, peaks never very high, but with magnificent changing panoramas, dry cistus, red-gold in the sunshine, masking rounded mountain tops and wide valleys to mingle with cork oaks, gnarled and old, and the dark myrtle among dry grasses. Around occasional hamlets clustered orchards, olive groves and patches of corn stubble, across tiny streams blackberry blossom still hung, and in the distance, once more, blue-shadowed heights lay one behind the other to a far horizon. Towards the top of Monte Maria gaunt rocks stand bleakly; there is said to have been a *nuraghe* here that was destroyed one night by lightning. It must have been an eerie scene in the raging storm on that isolated summit.

Up a steep rise the road curves round by a *cantonieri* house at the topmost point, before dropping down to Domusdemaria. I stopped the car to get out and look at this marvellous view. As I stood in the shadow of a small tree, from a ridge on the left a flock of goats appeared, making their slow, deliberate way, eventually reaching the bend opposite the house. There they stopped, though as I watched more and still more appeared. I had never seen such a herd. On and on they came, a veritable army of goats, black, white, grey, dark brown, light brown, skewbald, piebald, every possible variation of colour, and the Sardinian goat is a big, strong animal, the *caprone* often with splendid curving horns.

Presently they began to crowd the edge of the road. There was still no sight or sound of a shepherd, but all at once I realized what was happening. His forefeet on a hillock, a great golden tan *caprone* was governing the whole huge flock. Did a nanny get impatient, a small kid attempt to cross, the big beast swung his head in the direction of the offending animal, and once or twice gave a short, sharp, coughing grunt. He was immediately obeyed. It was a fantastic sight, and I was wondering how it was all going to end when in the distance, round the track from behind a rock, followed by a few stragglers, strode a man, covering the ground with the long, smooth lope of a mountain shepherd. As he came into sight he gave a thin, high whistle. The *caprone* jerked his head sharply towards the direction of the sound. Again came the signal, and without further ado the goat quietly stepped on to the road and led the herd across, to disappear down the hillside behind the *cantonieri* house.

A tall lean young man with a flashing smile, and black, dancing eyes beneath the sheltering peak of his cap, the *pastore* explained that this was a daily routine. There were now more than 400 in the herd, and every afternoon about this time they crossed to the valley below, to water. In the dawn he brought them back to the mountain grazing. How had he taught the big goat? The *pastore* shook his head with a smile of affectionate pride. 'He's a clever fellow that one. He didn't need teaching. He understood.'

I had been afraid that if I had crossed to the car for a camera and attempted to approach the leader it would disturb the whole scene, so had kept quite still. Now I promised myself to return, but I was never able to get there again at the right moment, though I saw the end of the procession again, twice.

Domusdemaria, an ancient village, lay shut in almost entirely on one side of the road, colour-washed cottages and an old church in a huddle together. Still further along the bend of the river Chia was a mass of pale oleanders and purple veronica bushes, leading to a pine forest and to Santa Margherita, and, down a long drive, right away from the road, the Is Morus hotel, my immediate destination, where I was looking forward to a brief respite before returning home.

Set among some 350 acres of pine and eucalyptus trees, with the mountains behind, the hotel faces the sea across a narrow garden full of flowers. Roses and heliotrope as well as more exotic blooms lead to three private beaches of white sand, and a natural shelf of pink rock slopes to the unbelievably blue water.

A long building of only two storeys, with two arms jutting towards the sea, which most of the rooms overlook, each with its own balcony, the Is Morus is not only my idea of holiday heaven, but apparently that of other guests, too, who from all over Europe and even further afield have returned year after year, ever since the hotel was first opened in 1958. The manager, Antonio Cappellari, is also Managing Director of SAIA, the company owning this and a smaller, cheaper hotel, the Villa del Parco, a couple of kilometres along the bay, in turn set in its own pine woods.

The first foreign hotelier to come to Sardinia, with experience on both sides of the Atlantic, Antonio Cappellari, born in Switzerland of an Italian family of hoteliers, combines the virtues of both countries—the efficiency of the Swiss, with the elegance and sensitivity of an Italian. The furniture is not 'hotel', there are garden flowers in the rooms, the service is excellent and multi-lingual—'sometimes we hardly know which language to speak'. Food and wine are good enough to please the most eclectic of tastes, served, except in the most unusual weather, on a sheltered terrace overlooking the gardens and that sea. Added to which in the hotel itself is peace. Television is a brief distance through the pines, at 'The Grill', set in the form of a hollow square round a dance floor under the trees. There is a swimming pool, and beach umbrellas, instead of the usual gaudy canvas versions, are made of eucalyptus branches. There are special facilities for children, and much, much more.

The Villa del Parco, managed by Alberto Cappellari, brother of Antonio, is smaller, half the price, simple and good. And in its grounds among the pines, served by well-made roads, are a number of villas, each in its own garden, among a profusion of flowers. A posse of *guardiani* keep constant watch for fire, and would-be purchasers of land are not only carefully vetted, but have to submit plans for building to be agreed with the Is Morus' own architect, a well-known Italian, Giovanni Cappabava.

The last days came, as last days will, outdoing, of course, all those other glorious sunny days, and even the moon nearly excelled that lovely, golden night a month earlier at Cagliari. This time a pearly sea met pearly sky, the moon a silver disc sending flickering diamonds of light across the water. Never had flowers smelled sweeter, the rasp of cicadas been more compelling.

Part Six

*

ORISTANO
AND ALGHERO

I was returning to London from Alghero, via Oristano, the first part of the route the same as to Barumini, until that confusing triangle when, instead of turning right, my way now led straight on, through the Campidano via Sanluri and Uras, past miles and miles of dark golden corn stubble, of *Prato Africano* threaded with wild pear trees. There was a very odd sky, to the south-west it seemed to reach right down to the earth, grey and forbidding, only an ancient *castello*, dark and ruined, on a peak rising abruptly from the plain, showed clear. On the opposite side of the road, to the north-east, it was much lighter, sunshine streaking a fringe of mountains on the horizon, poplars and eucalyptus trees, as ever, lining little streams, girdling old farmhouses painted apricot pink and yellow. As usual signposts left one guessing, all said Sassari, boldly enough, only one eventually admitting to Oristano, further to the east, when I was almost there.

At Uras a sudden bend in the road led into a grey stone village relieved only by the brilliant colours of doorways and window ledges. On rows of stone benches sat not only the usual old men, but this time, it seemed, most of the village. Doors and walls were bedecked with baskets for sale, expertly made of the ill-famed asphodel—among fields of which, legend has it, the dead of the ancients sought the Waters of Lethe—for oblivion. But it made good, strong baskets, the stripes of pale biscuit and darker brown being used very effectively. None of the baskets was made with a handle over the top, so I said a regretful 'No, thank you,' that would-be vendors took in good part. Grey skies, now heavier and even lower, perhaps emphasised an underlying sadness in the weary, malaria-tinged faces of older men and women, especially the latter. There was obviously not enough work, little money, but the villagers were as uninhibited and friendly as others, asking the usual questions, themselves responding with that *Sardo* smile, like a sudden light in a dark place.

The road skirts the lagoons and salt marshes of Arborea, and salt lakes on the outskirts of Oristano where fishermen are alleged still to use the same type of hooks as their neolithic forebears, and a primitive type of boat similar to those only now used in the Persian Gulf and in Peru. A couple of miles from Oristano itself is to be seen the austerely beautiful twelfth-century Pisan church of Santa Giusta. But this was not the moment to investigate, the storm had now broken, and through thunder and lightning as well as a deluge of hail I splashed my way into Oristano, to the Jolly hotel.

It was the usual Jolly, small, clean, simple, and sufficient. At lunch my waiter asked me where I came from, was I Swedish? No, I was English. Oh, he knew England, he had worked in Nottingham and Brighton for two years, also in the Isle of Man, but had never been to London as he had been warned that the cost of living was so high there.

About four o'clock the weather lightened, so I went out to look at Eleanora of Arborea's town. The warrior queen's statue stands on its high plinth outside the Palace of Justice, flanked by four lions, the scroll of the *Carta da Logu* in her hand.

Superficial observation confirmed Oristano as a busy, prosperous farming centre. Shops were displaying quantities of agricultural machinery, heavy gum boots and other stout footwear, animal foodstuffs and fertilisers, paint, harness, and hunting knives. In addition to familiar domestic commodities were more sophisticated goods such as beauty preparations from internationally famous firms such as Elizabeth Arden and Helena Rubinstein. There were Ronson lighters and underwater swimming outfits. Book shops indicated catholic tastes ranging from Karl Marx, Hegel, Truman Capote, Shakespeare and Dickens to Ian Fleming among whodunit authors, as well as religious writers.

In other windows, scattered among the plethora of bars, cafés and barbers' salons, were beautiful hand made laces—a local industry—for wedding dresses; while food shops offered a wide variety of branded articles as well as more familiar stocks. In a small, scrupulously clean food market set back from the road leading to the Jolly freshly caught fish were laid out artistically, meat and other farm produce looked good. A large branch of Upim, the Italian chain store, had some excellent merchandise and was being well patronised.

Among local townsfolk, moving purposefully on their errands, were countrymen and women, some of the latter in costume, this time consisting of the long, pleated skirt, here black, the usual beautifully embroidered white cotton blouse, a brocade bolero, and, on neat heads, a large white coif turned up and back from the face. I asked a trio if I might take a photograph of them, one, very young, with a pale virginal face such as one sees in early Italian paintings, another of the three I thought to be her mother. But they refused. Later I saw the third again, this time on the arm of an obvious husband. She said something as they saw me, and instantly his expression changed to proud antagonism. With a 'don't you dare' look on his face, he swept her past me. Not that I had had any intention of approaching her again, but I was sorry to have offended.

Date palms and magnolias galore among the ever-present oleanders spoke of heat, and in the heart of the town the thirteenth-century granite tower of St. Christopher, 150 feet high, built of big blocks of stone said to be without any bonding, was a reminder of earlier, warring days. In its square bulk, high up, hangs the big warning bell; at the sides, marks in the stones indicate where the tower had once been part of the encircling protective walls of the town. A strong double gate in the central arch was open, and chalked on one side were reminders of present tribulations—not the usual Communist slogan, but crossed hearts pierced with an arrow, above entwined initials.

From the tower a narrow street of old houses, some with lovely carved wooden doors and wrought iron balconies, led to the cathedral, seat of an Archbishop, and a separate sexagonal campanile roofed with multi-coloured tiles. In the mid-morning sunshine of the next day I returned to find an occupant of the doorstep of a side entrance over which are carved a Cardinal's hat and other insignia. It was a ragged man, stretched out, fast asleep. On the pillared steps of the cathedral itself sat a poor, witless woman, fiddling with a rosary and uttering pathetic, unintelligible pleas to the occasional passers-by entering the building.

On the last lap to Alghero I took the coast road. It was again a blustery day, alternating patterns of light and shade as clouds swept across the sky constantly changing the appearance of the landscape. Nearing Santa Caterina, just before dropping down to the sea, a small *nuraghe* stood alone on a knoll by the roadside in a dominating position. After it, on the opposite side, a long belt of afforestation was marked: '*Lavoro Publico—Oristano*'; then the pines changed to a eucalyptus plantation, the leaves shivering in the wind, by an imposing gateway at the side of which the flags of more than a dozen nations signified an international camping site. It was an ideal place.

Santa Caterina, high over pale cliffs at the edge of the sea, appeared to be engaged in a building orgy, brightly coloured bungalows sprouting in a veritable rash on the outskirts, among a few windswept trees.

Ancient in history, Cuglieri stands apart, spread over a hilltop. Below, the approach over a tumbling stream from the adjacent mountain, at the top, surrounded by a cluster of houses, is the old church, coloured tiles of the dome glinting in the sunlight, visible for miles. Though with an air of immense isolation the village is, indeed, at a crossroads leading to the centre of the island, as well as north and south. The position is superb: westward—facing the sea, eastward—the mountains, the air magnificent. And here again was the noticeably fine, clear skin of upland people.

Leaving Cuglieri, first a narrow road drops through olive and fig plantations, then rising, opens out to arrive at the village of Tresnuraghes, once more with stone benches outside houses, old men perched on them like a row of exhausted birds waiting for that last, long flight. Here, stone walls, looking as if they were built of blocks from *nuraghi*, were an unaccustomed feature, holding in check the small, grey cattle. Similarly, a little further on, lay Tinnura. And here, too, in the main streets were baskets, trays and other objects of the asphodel straw. And sitting in front of her home a young wife, hard at work. She showed me how it was done, the dry, not very long leaves have to be damped to make them supple, and from a tight central coil, whatever the object to be made, the asphodel is wound closely over a core of the grasses. The skill lies in pulling it tight enough to make a good and even job; it is tough and hard on the hands, a cow's horn shaved down to a fine point being necessary to thrust into a previous row in order to make a hole for the continuing row. This was no pretty job for delicate fingers, it was skilful work, the horn being firmly held in her fist, the thrust needing to be strong and certain. She said it took a day to make a small tray.

Down to Bosa the road was shocking, but only temporarily; the Italian government organization for assistance to backward regions, the *Cassa per il Mezzogiorno*, which is doing much to help Calabria, is also giving aid for roadwork in Sardinia. In pursuance of this the road to Alghero at this point was in the course of translation to a first-class *autostrada*, but such an eminently desirable condition was at that moment far from being achieved. As I picked a careful way over sharp granite, newly laid, not yet rolled, I heard a shrill whistle. Looking towards the direction from which the sound had come I found a group of roadmenders taking their midday break in the shelter of a huge tree. They laughed and waved, gesturing to show their sympathy. I waved back.

Bosa, down in a hollow, is proud of its river, the Temo, as being the only navigable one in Sardinia, also one of the longest.

By an old stone bridge in the centre of the town boats were moored, and along the bank on one side stood a row of strange, empty stone huts, evidence of some long past water traffic.

Climbing again, the road mounted by Villanova, this time on the final circuitous laps before dropping down to Alghero. But what a road! It swooped up and up, each curve revealing a different view of heights, fern-carpeted beneath gale-torn trees, granite outcrop thrusting through the short turf. It was primitive, solitary, strong. At the topmost point a flock of sheep stood in a huddle under a little group of stunted oaks, unmoving, tails to the wind, not giving the slightest sign of awareness of even the fierce barking of the shepherd's dog warning me to be off.

Concrete blockhouses marked the final passage of the road. Ahead, far below, in the misty blue bay lay the roofs of Alghero, beyond the port and Punto Giglio the famous Capo Caccia, the most westerly point of Sardinia, familiar to Spanish and other invaders, now better known for its Grotta di Nettuno, caves even larger than those at Cala Gonone, with marvellous stalagmites and stalactites, and in this age organized for tourists with regular trips, electric illuminations and other amenities.

Two hotels, the Capo Caccia and El Faro, situated in glorious positions either side of Porto Conte, the bay west of Alghero, have a special service of motor boats for visiting the grotto; but if the sea is rough it is always possible to enter from the landward side—if enough energy is forthcoming to descend and remount the *Escala del Cabriol*, 750 steps expertly laid winding from the cliff top to the grotto entrance.

On the eastern side of Capo Caccia the nearby green grotto rewards earlier risers: sunlight striking the water at an angle in the early morning is said to have a marvellous effect. Unhappily for me this grotto was closed for repairs at the time of my visit.

Alghero has become increasingly popular with visitors in recent years, with a local population of only 30,000, in 1966 some 193,000 tourists including about 73,000 Italians from the mainland came here for their holidays. The town itself is well worth exploring for besides the innumerable cafés, tourist shops, hotels and pensions large and small, and trattorias including a good, new one, two kilometres outside the city on the Sassari road called 'El Corral,' here is the stuff of history emphasised by ancient towers and walls.

Though there are many traces of former civilisations, as elsewhere throughout the island, the origins of Alghero so far remain unknown. Nothing is recorded prior to 1102 when, as a little fishing village, it became the property of the Doria family. From a variety of possibilities, including Roman, Arab and Spanish, today the generally accepted idea of the name is that it evolved from the quantities of seaweed deposited on the shores by incoming tides.

A young assistant of the local Director of Turism took me on a brief but patient tour of the Spanish section of the city, where Catalan is still spoken as the normal language. Indeed, Catalans and Sards in the town still do not mix, still speak their own languages, and when communication is necessary, use Italian.

We inspected the early fifteenth-century Spanish-Gothic cathedral with its pillared portico and handsome baroque pulpit among other interesting details, then wandered through the old streets with their Catalan arches, and Catalan names such as the via Majorca, and Barcelonetta. On the ramparts are old houses, and the *Torre di Cane*, where stray dogs are collected rather than let them run starving in the streets. We stood looking down on the busy port; near at hand a bunch of coral fishing boats were preparing to put out, beyond, in a special section, private craft, motor boats and small yachts, were at safe anchor.

When Alghero was still a walled city, in fact, until not much more than a hundred years ago, here above the port was one of the four gates in the city walls. At this and the three other entrances at eleven o'clock every night, from the topmost ledge of each gate a guard would call, in Catalan, 'Who is without, stays out. Those within, stay inside.' And the gates would then be closed against the night and all comers.

Towards sunset I drove to Fertilia, the airport, to catch the late BEA flight direct to England. The wind had dropped and in the calm air the sun sank slowly, leaving flaming rose-red and orange streamers reaching far out into the sky. Presently we took off, the steward changed into his white jacket, and somebody said: 'We're away.'

The Viscount climbed higher and higher, and as I watched, the last rays of red and gold clung to the horizon for a long time, as though reluctant to let this day go.

Appendix 1

*

HOW TO GET THERE

BY AIR

British European Airways have one direct Flight a week—B212 —to and from Alghero, leaving London on Sunday night. The return Flight is on Saturday evening. Both journeys are by Viscount.

Connections can also be made at Rome, Milan or Genoa on daily Flights from and to London, the final leg of the journey connecting with Alghero or Cagliari being made by Alitalia domestic airlines. For the daily connection with Alghero it is necessary to fly to Rome and change there.

In the season there are several Flights daily by Alitalia to both Alghero and Cagliari.

During the season special day tourist excursion fares are valid for mid-week travel only. From April 1st to June 15th, and October 1st to 31st they are available on any day.

For Flights to Olbia—for the *Costa Smeralda*—there are special connections at Milan and Rome, for which a supplement is payable.

BY SHIP

The *Tirrenia* line operates ferries daily to and from:

Civitavecchia – Olbia
Civitavecchia – Cagliari
Genoa   – Porto Torres
        and
Naples   – Cagliari on Sundays and Wednesdays, the return journeys being Mondays and Thursdays.

Also the *Canguro Rosso* line from:

Genoa	– Cagliari on Mondays and Fridays, the return journeys being Tuesdays and Saturdays.
Genoa	– Olbia on Wednesday, returning the next day.

Appendix 2

✳

HOTELS

Place	Class	Hotel	No. of Rooms & Beds
ALGHERO	I	Capo Caccia	116 – 232
	I	Dei Pini	82 – 160
	I	El Faro	80 – 150
	I	E.S.I.T. (Grand Hotel)	57 – 93
	I	Villa Las Tronas	38 – 68
	II	Casablanca	46 – 88
	II	Continental	32 – 63
	II	Coral	22 – 40
	II	Eleonora	60 – 115
	II	La Lepanto	40 – 55
	II	La Margherita	58 – 105
	II	Mediterraneo	43 – 79
	II	Miramare	36 – 64
	II	Park Hotel	53 – 104
	II	San Marco	57 – 97
	II	Tarragona	39 – 65
	III	Helvetia	23 – 42
	III	Internazionale	24 – 48
	III	Lido	25 – 45
ARITZO	III	Moderno	30 – 54
ARZACHENA (Costa Smeralda)	I	Cala di Volpe	40 – 60
	I	Cervo	62 – 124
	I	Pitrizza	27 – 52
	I	Romazzino	100 – 200
ARZACHENA	II	Laconia	52 – 104
	II	Motel—Tuf-Tuf	33 – 66
	III	Ringo	20 – 40
	III	Sa Berritta	14 – 28
BITTIA	III	Dell' Annunziata	13 – 19
CAGLIARI	I	Enlac	56 – 112
	I	E.S.I.T. Al Poetto	114 – 207
	I	Jolly Regina Margherita	130 – 191
	II	Capo Sant'Elia	44 – 75

195

Place	Class	Hotel	No. of Rooms & Beds
CAGLIARI	II	Excelsior-Miramare	46 – 76
	II	Mediterraneo	148 – 241
	II	Moderno	80 – 110
	III	Italia	90 – 145
	III	Motel AGIP	57 – 114
CARBONIA	III	Centrale	37 – 50
CARLOFORTE	II	Riviera	28 – 46
CAPOTERA	II	Giber	16 – 31
CASTELDORIA TERME	II	Terme di Casteldoria	36 – 44
DORGALI	III	Bue Marino	34 – 57
	III	Miramare	18 – 32
	III	Miramare (Dipendenza)	14 – 26
GOLFO DEGLI ARANCI	II	Margherita	25 – 46
IGLESIAS	II	Hotel Artu	22 – 31
LA MADDELENA	II	E.S.I.T.	25 – 42
	II	Excelsior	33 – 50
	III	Al Mare	29 – 52
	III	Nido d'Aquila	16 – 20
LAMPIANU (Sassari)	II	Villaggio Nurra	66 – 132
MACOMER	II	Motel AGIP	30 – 60
	III	Stazione	20 – 29
NUORO	I	Jolly	45 – 61
	II	E.S.I.T. (Monte Ortobene)	53 – 82
	III	Da Giovanni	13 – 25
OLBIA	I	Abi d'Oru	60 – 102
	I	Jolly	44 – 52
	II	Caprile	27 – 51
	II	Motel Olbia	20 – 40
	III	Gallura	25 – 44
	III	Italia	13 – 21
	III	Mastino	21 – 35
	III	Minerva	41 – 64
ORISTANO	II	Hotel del Sole	54 – 96
	II	Jolly Standard	50 – 71
	III	Piccolo	16 – 16

Place	Class	Hotel	No. of Rooms & Beds
OZIERI	III	Mastino	42 – 59
PALAU	II	Excelsior Vanna	32 – 60
	II	La Roccia	20 – 40
	II	Porto Pollo	24 – 48
	III	Serra	16 – 32
PLATAMONA LIDO	I	Pontinental	149 – 266
PORTOSCUSO	III	Panorama	27 – 54
	III	S'Alegusta	50 – 80
PORTO TORRES	III	Da Elisa	12 – 20
SANT'ANNA ARRESI	III	Portopino Motel	31 – 62
SANTA LUSSURGIU	II	E.S.I.T. San Leonardo	29 – 49
	II	E.S.I.T. San Leonardo (Dipendenza)	6 – 10
	II	E.S.I.T. San Leonardo (Dipendenza—2)	3 – 5
SANTA MARGHERITA DI PULA	I	Is Morus	55 – 96
	II	Villa del Parco	21 – 38
SANTA TERESA GALLURA	I	Moresco	53 – 100
	II	E.S.I.T. Miramare	16 – 34
	II	Il. Gallo di Gallura	85 – 150
	II	Tibula	63 – 105
	III	Bella Vista	16 – 26
	III	Canne al Vento	12 – 16
	III	Cristina	15 – 22
	III	Moderno	18 – 30
	III	Quattro Mori	10 – 20
	III	Smeraldo	15 – 30
	III	Sole e Mar	20 – 37
SAN TEODORO	III	Elios	17 – 27
SASSARI	I	Jolly Grazia Deledda	140 – 228
	II	Jolly Hotel	59 – 79
	II	Motel AGIP	57 – 114
	II	Motel La Giocca	40 – 80
	III	Castello	33 – 51
	III	Gallura	21 – 36
	III	Sardegna	27 – 38
	III	Turritania	92 – 135

Place	Class	Hotel	No. of Rooms & Beds
SINISCOLA	II	La Caletta	64 – 125
	II	La Caletta (Dipendenza)	48 – 81
	II	Villa Pozzi	50 – 100
SORGONO	II	E.S.I.T. Villa Fiorita	20 – 35
STINTINO	II	Grand Hotel Rocca Ruja	107 – 214
TEMPIO PAUSANIA	II	E.S.I.T. Miramonti	42 – 73
	II	Petit Hotel	49 – 98
	II	Vallicciola	20 – 35
	III	Villa Conconi	12 – 24
TONARA	II	E.S.I.T. Noccioleto	21 – 41
TORTOLI	III	Speranza	24 – 43
	III	Splendor	17 – 28
	III	Victoria	40 – 54
VILLACIDRO	II	E.S.I.T. La Spendula	15 – 26
VILLASIMIUS	I	Grand Hotel Capo Boi	103 – 205
	II	Timi-Ama Residence Hotel	32 – 64

In addition to the hotels listed above there are a number designated as 4th class, as well as some pensions, details of which can be obtained from the London or Sardinian offices of the State Tourist organizations, or from Travel Agents. The Hotel Romazzino on the *Costa Smeralda* is one of the Rank Organization properties. Particulars can be obtained from that Company at 11 Belgrave Road, London, S.W.1 as well as from the hotel direct.

The majority of hotels and pensions are open for a specific period during the year, generally from the beginning of May to the end of September, and it is worth enquiring as to this when considering a stay.

Buying Land and Villas

In addition, information regarding the purchase of land or villas, or the renting of furnished villas can be obtained from:

The Costa Smeralda Information Office
109 Kingsway, London, W.C.1.

and

Anglo Italiana Ltd. (for Punta Sardegna Properties)
14 Cockspur Street, London, W.1.

or

Miss Mary Bayntun,
Anglo Italiana Ltd.,
Punta Sardegna, Palau, Sardinia.

or

Mrs Anne Bassett,
Punta Sardegna, Palau, Sardinia.

Under present regulations, in the case of these two firms, transactions being in sterling make possible either the purchase of land or villas, or the temporary renting of villas.

Arrangements for the purchase of land on the SAIA (Is Morus Hotel) property, and elsewhere from other Italian companies can only be made at present with permission from the Bank of England.

Camping Sites

There are camping sites available, and here again, details of conditions as well as lists of the villages are best obtained in the first instance from the State Tourist offices.

Club Mediterranee

The Club Mediterranee have a village at Caprera. Particulars of membership can be obtained from the offices of this body at 40 Conduit Street, London, W.1. And in this connection it is worth noting that a special arrangement has now been made with British European Airways for Group Travel for members of this organization direct from London to Alghero which offers a considerable saving over ordinary rates.

Index

Adelphi Terrace, 43
Africa, 30, 40, 73, 175. *See also* Tunisia
Aga Khan, 20, 21, 25
Aggius, 45, 48
Agincourt Sound, 33, 35
Albo mountains, 82
Alfonso IV of Spain, 148
Alghero, 14–16, 50, 66, 102, 112, 184, 187–90
Alitalia, 14
America, North, 19, 40, 41
America, South, 40
Antine, Sant', 66, 67, 162
Antioco, San, 167, 170, 178
Arab, 120, 165, 190
Aragon, 49, 148, 149
Arancia, Golfo di, 24
Arbatax, 140, 141
Arborea, 19, 148, 185
Aristotle, 13
Aritzo, 96, 125, 128–9, 136
Armosino, Francesca, 44
Arzachena, 20, 27, 30
Asinara, Gulf of, 54–5, 64–5
Asuai, 131
Atlantic, 62
Australia, 40
Austrians, 19, 39, 40, 43

Bacchiddu, Dr, 75, 81
Baker, Josephine, 31
Balestieri, Punta, 46
Bandits, 104–6, 111–114
Barbary Coast, 34
Bari Sardo, 140
Barumini, 47, 161–2, 165, 184
Bavaria, 149
Beales, 43
Bellavista, Capo, 141
Belvi, 71, 129, 133, 137, 140

Bidighinzu, 69, 140
Bithia, 148
Black Sea, 23, 62
Blackwood, Sir Henry, 35, 36
Boadicea, 149
Boi, Capo, 159
Bonifacio, Straits of, 29
Bonnanaro, 66
Bosa, 188
Bourbon, 38
British European Airways, 14, 190
Brunas, Padre Vittorio, 64
Bruncu Spina, 127
Busiri Vici, Michele, 20, 29
Byzantines, 19, 148

Caccia, Capo, 189
Cagliari, 19, 45, 49, 50, 56, 66, 71, 73, 86, 107, 118, 123, 131–2, 137, 140–1, 145–6, 147–9, 150–2, 155, 158–9, 161–2, 165, 167, 172, 183
Cala di Volpi, Hotel, 25
Cala Gonone, 98–9, 121, 189
Calabria, 24, 57, 161, 188
Calasetta, 178
Campidano, 86, 156, 162, 165, 184
Cannas river, 146
Cannonau wine, 54
Capo Boi, Hotel, 160
Cappabava, Giovanni, 182
Caprera, 29, 33, 36–9, 40–1
Caralis, 148, 155. *See also* Karales
Carbonara, Capo, 147, 160
Carbonia, 166
Carlo Alberto, 150
Carlo Emmanuele III, 54, 170
Carlo Felice, 150, 152
Carloforte, 169, 170, 176
Carta da Logu, 149, 152, 185
Carta da Musica, 82, 108